ART ADVENTURES

A Curriculum Guide for Home Schools

LEVEL 2

An intermediate art program geared toward the upper elementary grades

by M. Jean Soyke

illustrated by Pattye Carlson

Printed and distributed by At Home Publications
Forest Hill, Maryland 21050
www.athomepubs.com

July 2006 printing
ISBN:0-9754142-2-4

TABLE OF CONTENTS

Introduction 1

How to Use This Book 1

Objectives From Level 1 3

Sample Lesson Plan 4

Why Art? 5

Teaching Art 6

Materials Needed for Teaching Art 9

Curriculum 11

Objectives for Level 3 11

Year A Projects 13

Year B Projects 63

Year C Projects 105

The Art Field Trip 125

Glossary 139

Bibliography 149

Index 151

INTRODUCTION

HOW TO USE THIS BOOK

About the Program

Art Adventures at Home is a total art curriculum for children in the elementary grades. The curriculum section of each book presents a three-year art program, with 35 lessons per year. All of the objectives for each level are presented in the first year, while activities in the second and third years reinforce the concepts already introduced. Most people will want to do one art lesson per week, perhaps supplementing with art activities related to other subject areas, seasonal crafts, and/or art-related field trips.

Grade Placement

The lessons for this volume are written for students who are beginning third, fourth, or fifth grades. However, parents should look over the objectives from Level 1 on page 3 to determine if their child has already mastered those concepts and vocabulary. If not, it may be wise to complete the first year of Level 1 before beginning this volume.

Parents with several children may wish to place those in grades K-2 together, those in grades 3-5 together, and those in grades 6-8 together. Each group can then begin at their appropriate level and continue their art instruction together throughout their elementary years. Since the same five units are covered each year, parents with children on different levels will be able to teach art to all their children at the same time, using the same materials but with different activities and/or objectives.

Teaching the Lessons

Each lesson in Art Adventures at Home is designed to be followed step-by-step. It is recommended that you read each lesson thoroughly before it is to be presented, perhaps even trying the project first to make sure the process is understood. (There is a description of a lesson plan on page 4 to give you an idea of what each section of the lesson involves.) If all the necessary materials are gathered, prepared, and organized ahead of time, the art lesson will go much more smoothly.

Although this curriculum is highly structured, there is plenty of room for flexibility. For example, blank lesson plans are included at the end of each year so that you can design your own lessons, if you wish. It is recommended that you teach Year A exactly as written, but you may want to switch a lesson in Year B with a lesson in Year C that covers the same objective. We do not recommend that you change the order of the lessons within a unit; however, the order of the *units* may be changed during any given year. (We have placed a line on each page to write the date; this will help you keep track of any changes that you make.) Even though the program is well-structured, please remember that it is only a tool. Let your child's readiness and interest dictate the course of your instruction. Feel free to omit a lesson if your child is totally frustrated or uninterested, or change the focus of the lesson if your child is interested in a different aspect of it. Let this curriculum serve your needs!

Some of the lessons suggest that the child look at particular samples of art. At the request of many parents, we have compiled several of these into a convenient set that we call the Masterpak, which can be used for all three years of this program. Please see the form at the back of this book for ordering information. If you would prefer to find the samples yourself or to investigate a particular artist or medium in more depth, usually an encyclopedia or the Internet will yield useful examples. A visit to the art history section of your public library may also prove fruitful. A resourceful parent who plans ahead should have little difficulty in finding appropriate samples for these art lessons.

We have confidence that this curriculum will not only enable you to teach your child the fundamentals of art, but it will also provide some fun, challenging, and rewarding experiences for your family.

OBJECTIVES FROM LEVEL 1

ART ELEMENTS	CONCEPTS
Line	Lines can create shapes. (L1) Lines can suggest action and movement. (L2) Lines can create texture and detail. (L3) Lines can be used to express an idea. (L4) Lines can show various emotions. (L5) Lines can be repeated to create rhythm. (L6)
Shape/Form	Shapes can be repeated to suggest movement. (S1) Shapes can be combined to make objects. (S2) Shapes can be repeated to create patterns. (S3) Large shapes emphasize an object's importance. (S4) Shapes can be repeated to unify a design. (S5) Forms can be representational or non-representational. (F1) Forms can be useful (crafts). (F2) Forms have roundness. (F3)
Color	Colors can be mixed to make new colors. (C1) Colors can be warm or cool. (C2) Colors can suggest a mood. (C3) Colors can be repeated to create patterns. (C4) Colors can be repeated to unify a design. (C5)
Texture	Texture adds detail and interest. (T1) Textures can be very smooth to very rough. (T2) Textures can be visual or tactile. (T3) Textures can be repeated to unify a design. (T4)

SAMPLE LESSON PLAN

LESSON FORMAT **(Title)** **Date** ____________

BIG IDEA: This is the art concept being taught. *(See page 11.)*

GOAL: This tells how the child will demonstrate his knowledge of the concept in a particular art project.

MAIN ELEMENTS: This tells which of the four elements of art is emphasized (line, shape/form, color, or texture)

MATERIALS: This section lists all of the art materials you will need.

STRATEGY:

This is the **teaching** section of the lesson. It describes exactly how to prepare the child for the art project. Generally, some ideas for motivating the child are given first, then suggestions are given for presenting and discussing the concept. These are followed by step-by-step instructions for demonstrating the technique.

WORK PERIOD:

This is the **learning** section of the lesson. It tells exactly what the child will be doing, including specific directions for the child to demonstrate the concept being emphasized.

QUESTIONS FOR EVALUATION AND REVIEW:

Specific questions are given for you to ask the child. Some questions will help you determine the child's understanding of the concept and technique being taught. Other questions encourage self-evaluation and introduce techniques of art appreciation.

WHY ART?

In the beginning, God gave an amazing gift whose only purpose was to bring pleasure. The gift is evident in the design, form, textures, and vibrant hues we see in nature-- the animal kingdom, mountain ranges, flowers, gems, jungles, and the ever-changing sky. The gift is beauty. It has the power to stir our emotions, renew and refresh us, and stretch our imaginations. When we experience *art*, we participate in the same creative process, and in this way receive and reflect back to our Creator the gift of beauty.

Yet, for teachers and parents, art is more than the means through which beauty is created. Art education is a valuable tool, for it reinforces learning through multisensory experiences. It is especially suited for visual and kinesthetic learners-- those who learn best by seeing and doing-- while benefitting auditory and kinesthetic learners by increasing skills in visual perception. Furthermore, art education is a useful tool for developing:

- sensory perception (ability to see, understand, gain meaning)
- thinking skills (examine, compare, evaluate, analyze, solve problems)
- communication of thoughts and feelings
- positive self-regard as successes are experienced in creating beauty
- an increased capacity for enjoying beauty

Sadly, at different times and places, movements have arisen in protest of art. For example, the Dark Ages was a period in history when beauty and creativity were suppressed in all forms. As parents teaching art, however, we look to the Creator as our example. He is the first and ultimate Artist; color, line, shape, form, texture-- all are His design. From the Garden of Eden, to the purple and scarlet fabrics of the "excellent wife", to the heavenly streets of precious stone, God has revealed Himself as a God of beauty. Beauty is His gift to us; it is in His image that we are made creative. Being stewards of beauty and creativity means that we acknowledge and enjoy His creation and use these gifts to develop ourselves and our children as art is so uniquely suited to do.

TEACHING ART

If we are indeed stewards of the creativity God has given us, how do we convey this to our children? How can our art lessons encourage children to express their creativity in a purposeful manner? Perhaps the right way to teach art can best be discovered by exploring some *wrong* ways to teach art.

Giving the child pre-designed materials

It makes life much simpler when we can hand an adult-designed craft kit to a child and call it "art class". The truth of the matter is, however, that "art" such as this requires little thought or creativity on the part of the student. The child is not free to stretch his imagination, learn about new materials or processes, express an idea or share what has been perceived. We must even be careful in choosing projects that must be done "just so"; although certain art processes have definite procedures, there must be room left for the child to plan how he will arrive at the end product he has designed. Studies have shown that pre-planned "art" actually inhibits creativity and causes children to regress in their ability to express themselves artistically.

Over-emphasizing neatness

Some of us may become a bit anxious when we consider the potential mess an art project can bring, but we need to be careful not to limit our projects to neat and tidy ones. Several things can be done to minimize the mess associated with the creative process. First, demonstrate individual techniques with neatness in mind. When using glue, for example, demonstrate how to apply glue with a fingertip, teaching your child that "a little dab will do ya". It is also important to show young painters how to remove excess paint from their brushes by drawing the brush along the lip of the paint container. Second, develop a clean-up routine. One rule that may help is "hands are washed before smocks come off".

As far as the finished product is concerned, we should encourage a child to do his best work, but should also accept a project even if the edges are slightly askew, or the paint ran a little. Placing too high a priority on neatness can actually inhibit our child's creativity and lower his self-esteem.

Giving too little direction

We've already explained how an art teacher can unwittingly inhibit creativity. This does not mean, however, that you should just give your child some art materials with some instructions and then go off and do the laundry. Studies have shown that children left completely to themselves in the art realm become frustrated, bored, and/or discouraged. The key to good art instruction is a balance of freedom and direction. Your child should be in control of the ideas and the development of the project; he also needs freedom to explore ways in which he might reach the goal he has selected for his project. When your child comes to a "dead end", however, you need to be there to offer assistance. Avoid giving answers; ask questions and encourage your child to solve his own problems. There may also be times when you may need to re-teach a step or method. As you work through some art projects together, you will learn how to guide your child through an art experience that is both satisfying and challenging.

There is also something to be said for doing an art project along with your child. Not only are you available for assistance and direction, but you will have a good sense of any rough spots that the child may encounter in the process of executing the project. Working alongside another is also a wonderful facilitator of communication. Both children and adults are often amazingly willing to open up and share personal thoughts while their hands are occupied (hence the popularity of the old-fashioned "quilting bees"). In addition, you are conveying an important message to your child that art is both a pleasurable and worthwhile activity. (There is one danger in this approach, however. You may need to "hide" or abandon your project if you discover that your child is measuring the value of his project by comparing it to yours.)

Passing judgment on your child's art

"How do you like my painting?" our child asks, and we, being proud and enthusiastic parents, exclaim, "That's beautiful-- wonderful-- really great!" As natural as this is to do, our children need us to resist the urge to respond this way automatically. Since one of our goals is to help our children develop an intrinsic appreciation of their art, we must bear in mind that continuous praise may easily lead a child to use his art merely as a means of gaining approval. We can give more helpful feedback by responding, "Tell me about your painting," or "How do *you* feel about your drawing?" Your child may share an imaginative story to explain what's going on in the work. Or, maybe he will express frustration in a certain area, thus giving you the opportunity to facilitate some problem-solving. Once you've listened to your child's thoughts, it is often meaningful to give a compliment that is a specific, simple observation: "I see you chose all oranges and reds; it really gives your picture a warm feeling," or "The way you repeat this shape really makes for an interesting pattern." This will reinforce the concepts being learned, facilitate intrinsic appreciation, and help prevent praise-dependency.

A word about grading

You may be in a situation where you are required to present a "grade" for your child's art work. It is *not* appropriate to grade solely on the appearance of the final project, nor is it appropriate to give children letter grades for art. The following questions can help you arrive at your final assessment of the project.

- Did the student meet the basic goal as stated in the lesson plan?
- Did the student strive toward good craftsmanship?
- Does the project express a new perspective or original thought?

With these obstacles removed, your child's natural creativity will flow more freely in your art sessions. Offer your support. Help your child slow down long enough to *see*. Pique interest with trips to museums and unusual places to draw. Provide a variety of supplies and plenty of opportunity to use them. Most important, discuss design and beauty as it pertains to the things they experience every day. This type of an art program will develop an inner sensitivity and enjoyment of art that will impact your child for life.

MATERIALS USED IN TEACHING ART

Items to Buy

☐ Waterproof smock

☐ Paint brushes (various widths)

☐ Water color markers

☐ Heavy tacky glue (for fabric crafts)

☐ Crayons (64-pack)

☐ White paper in varying sizes

☐ Ruler

☐ Sand (plain and colored)

☐ Plaster of Paris

☐ Nylon craft loops (for potholders)

☐ Sandpaper of varying textures

☐ Oil-based paints (for marbling paper)

☐ Drinking straws

☐ Fabric paints *(Year C only)*

☐ Fabric dye *(Year B only)*

☐ Colored tissue paper *(Year C only)*

☐ Construction paper of varying colors

☐ Glue stick and white "school" glue

☐ Adult-quality scissors with blunt tips

☐ Self-hardening clay

☐ Mod Podge® craft gloss

☐ Metylan® instant wallpaper paste, for papier mâché

☐ Oil pastel crayons

☐ Masking tape

☐ Free-standing mirror

☐ Single hole punch

☐ Turpentine or mineral spirits *(Year B)*

☐ Large balloon *(Year C)*

☐ Glue gun *(optional)*

☐ Clear Contact® paper *(optional)*

☐ Easel *(optional)*

☐ Kneaded eraser (available from art supply stores; used in Year C, but handy to have for many other art projects)

☐ Heavy-duty aluminum foil or aluminum pie pans

☐ Liquid tempera paints (red, blue, black, brown, magenta, green, yellow, white. Get twice as much of the yellow and white- they are used more and tend to run out more quickly.) You may also wish to buy a separate paint cup and brush for each color, especially if you are using an easel. A styrofoam egg carton is good for table work.

Items to Collect

☐ Old magazines and newspapers

☐ Fabric and felt scraps

☐ Old sponges

☐ Old toothbrushes

☐ Plastic container for water

☐ Styrofoam plates (for mixing paint colors)

☐ Styrofoam egg cartons (for paints)

☐ Old tube sock (for puppet- Year A only)

☐ Yarn and rope in various colors

☐ Styrofoam meat trays

☐ Old manila folders or tagboard

☐ Cardboard boxes & tubes (all sizes)

☐ Small jars with lids

☐ Old crayons or candles for melting

☐ Flat pieces of cardboard

☐ Plastic ring from a six-pack of soda

☐ Miscellaneous dried foods (ex., such as beans or pasta)

☐ Gadgets for rubbings or clay work (ex., nuts and bolts, buttons, coins, lace, pasta shapes, feathers, leaves, bark, chains, combs, pebbles, checkers, paper clips, hair pins, shells, pine cones, acorn, etc.)

☐ Tools for etching (ex., toothpick, nutpick, nail, old pen, screwdriver, straightened paper clip, bobby pin)

☐ Gadgets to use as painting tools (ex., evergreen branch, marble, toy car, cotton ball, leaf, fork, soda straw, feather, etc.)

CURRICULUM

OBJECTIVES

The following list outlines the basic concepts that are taught in this curriculum. Each lesson plan will cover one or more of these concepts, although not necessarily in this order. If you are developing your own lesson plans, you will want to refer back to this list to make sure all of the material is covered. (NOTE: All of these objectives are covered each year.)

ART ELEMENTS	CONCEPTS
Line	Lines can represent mass. (L1) Lines have contour; they are thick or thin. (L2) Lines vary, depending on tool and medium. (L3) Lines can repeat and form patterns. (L4)
Shape/Form	Shapes occur in our environment and can be organic or man-made. (S1) Detail can emphasize main shapes. (S2) Shapes can influence feelings and attitudes. (S3) Overlapping shapes can create an illusion of space. (S4) Forms occur in our environment and can be organic or man-made. (F1)
Color	Colors have complements. (C1) Colors can be neutral. (C2) A color's value can be changed by adding white (tints) or black (shades). (C3) Colors can be blended or swirled. (C4) Colors can be affected by adjacent colors. (C5) Colors can create contrast (ex., light-dark, bright-dull). (C6) Repeated colors can create rhythm. (C7)
Texture	Textures vary, depending on medium and tool. (T1) Repeated textures can create rhythm. (T2)

YEAR A - PROJECTS

Unit I - Drawing

1. Line Design
2. Still Life
3. Textured Drawings
4. Story Picture
5. Crayon Etching
6. Shape Design
7. Something Special

Unit II - Print-Making

8. Nature Prints
9. Mock Stained Glass
10. Crayon Tracing
11. Gadget Printing
12. Aluminum Pan Print
13. Collograph I
14. Collograph II

Unit III - Painting

15. Color Mixing
16. Oil Pastel Resist
17. Non-Representational Design
18. Chalk Resist
19. Tempera Batik
20. Experimenting With a Variety of Paints
21. Experimenting With a Variety of Painting Tools

Unit IV - Sculpture

22. Introduction to Clay
23. Clay Animals I
24. Clay Animals II
25. Sculpture from Found Objects I
26. Sculpture from Found Objects II
27. Sand and Plaster Bas Relief I
28. Sand and Plaster Bas Relief II

Unit V - Crafts

29. Paper Placemat
30. Finger Weaving
31. Sand Painting
32. Coil Pot I
33. Coil Pot II
34. Sock Puppet
35. Wrapping Paper

SAMPLES OF LINE

LESSON 1, YEAR A **Line Design** **Date** ______________

BIG IDEA: Lines can repeat and form patterns. (L4)

GOAL: The child will create a line design, using repeating lines to form a pattern.

MAIN ELEMENTS: Line

MATERIALS:

Pencil or dark-colored marker (black, blue, brown, or purple)
White paper, 8½ X 11 or smaller
Ruler

STRATEGY:

• Review with your child different types of line (wavy, curved, jagged, etc.). *(See facing page for samples of different kinds of line.)*

• Look around your house for patterns that are created by repeating lines. (These could be found on clothing, wallpaper, lineoleum floors, carpet, dishes, etc.). Have your child identify the basic line(s) and tell how the pattern was created. (For example, this pattern- ⌇ ⌇ ⌇ ⌇ ⌇ ⌇ - is created by repeating wavy lines.)

WORK PERIOD:

• Have your child use a ruler to divide a sheet of paper into four to eight large areas.

• In each area, the child should create a pattern, using repeating lines. (There should be a different pattern in each section, and each area should be totally filled.)

QUESTIONS FOR EVALUATION AND REVIEW:

What different kinds of lines did you use in each section?

How did you create the pattern in each section? *(by repeating lines)*

Which pattern do you like best? Which do you think is the most interesting? Why?

LESSON 2, YEAR A **Still Life** **Date** ______________

BIG IDEA: Lines can represent mass. (L1)

GOAL: The child will draw an arrangement of objects, using different lines to represent mass.

MAIN ELEMENT: Line

MATERIALS:

Magazine pictures, artists' sketches, or comic strips (black and white preferred)
Paper
Pencil

STRATEGY:

• Select pictures that show objects of different mass. Ask your child to identify the kinds of line that are used to depict each object. Help him see that thicker lines tend to define objects that are heavy, and thinner lines are used to depict lighter objects.

WORK PERIOD:

• Have your child arrange a still life of toys, kitchen utensils, tools, or an area of the room. The still life should include objects of differing masses, such as large and heavy, small and delicate.

• The child draws the still life, varying lines to represent the different masses.

QUESTIONS FOR EVALUATION AND REVIEW:

Look at each object in the still life. What line(s) did you choose to show how heavy or light each object is?

How do you feel about the drawing?

LESSON 3, YEAR A **Textured Drawing** **Date** ______________

BIG IDEA: Textures vary, depending on medium and tool. (T1)

GOAL: The child will make a simple drawing on different types of paper to see how texture can vary.

MAIN ELEMENT: Texture

MATERIALS:

Pencil
White paper of at least three different textures (ex., white construction paper, regular bond paper, tissue paper, wallpaper- even fine sand-paper! Many art supply stores also carry single sheets of textured paper in textures unavailable at home.)

STRATEGY:

• Have your child examine the different kinds of paper. Help him describe the different textures. (If he is interested, he may want to find out how the different papers are made to create the different textures.)

• Explain that we can change the texture of a drawing by changing the paper we use.

WORK PERIOD:

• Have your child choose a **simple** item to draw.

• Have your child select a paper and draw the item on it. (He does not need to add a lot of detail to this drawing.)

• Have your child select a different texture of paper and repeat the drawing. Have him do this a third time with a different texture of paper.

QUESTIONS FOR EVALUATION AND REVIEW:

How did the texture of the paper affect your drawing?

Which paper was the easiest to draw on? The hardest?

Which paper created the most interesting picture? The least interesting?

Which paper, do you think, created the best texture for the item you were drawing?

BIG IDEA: Overlapping shapes can create the illusion of space. (S4)

GOAL: The child will make a line drawing, using overlapping shapes to create the illusion of space.

MAIN ELEMENT: Shape

MATERIALS:

Magazine pictures
Paper
Crayons or markers
Three or four cut-out paper shapes (preferably of different colors)

STRATEGY:

• Look at the magazine pictures with your child. Ask, "Which thing is in front of the others? How do you know?" The child should point out that the closer object overlaps the others.

• Show your child the paper shapes. Put one shape partly over another and ask, "Which shape looks closer to you?" Point out that overlapping the shapes makes one appear closer than the other. (If your child needs more work with this concept, allow him to experiment with the different paper shapes.)

• Have your child overlap two of the paper shapes and practice drawing them. Remind him to draw just the parts of the shapes that he **sees**, not the parts that are hidden. Repeat until your child is able to reproduce the shapes fairly accurately.

• Explain that drawing a story is different from drawing a still life. "You will be drawing a picture from your imagination. You will not be drawing something you are seeing with your eyes."

• Discuss what kind of story your child would like to draw. Some possible titles might be: "My Best Day Ever", "When I'm Grown Up", "Last Night I Dreamed...", "My Vacation", "My Day at the Zoo", or "My Birthday Party".

• Encourage your child to draw the story, using overlapping shapes to give the impression of depth. Your child should fill the page, using large strokes with lots of detail.

WORK PERIOD:

• The child decides on a story and a title, then draws the story. (NOTE: With large drawing paper, children manage best with the paper attached to an easel or wall.)

QUESTIONS FOR EVALUATION AND REVIEW:

Tell me what is happening in your story. What do you like about your drawing?

BIG IDEA: Lines have contour; they are thick or thin. (L2)

GOAL: The child will work with lines of varying contour in a crayon etching.

MAIN ELEMENT: Line

MATERIALS:

Smock
Newspaper
Paper, prepared by drawing an 8" X 10" rectangle on it
Crayons
Black tempera paint (or other dark color)
Liquid soap detergent
Etching tools of varying thicknesses (ex., toothpick, nutpick, nail, old pen, straightened paper clip, flat-head screwdriver)

STRATEGY:

• Explain the concept: "Lines can be thick or thin. This is called **contour**."

• Explain the etching process: "First we'll color our paper with crayons. We can use only one color or lots of different colors. *(Demonstrate how to color using heavy strokes.)* Next we'll cover our paper with paint. When the paint is dry, we will scratch out lines so that the color shows through. This is called 'etching'."

• Help your child select a subject or scene that would require lines of different thickness. You may wish to review the concept from Lesson 2 by having your child choose objects of different masses. (For example, a garden might have light, delicate flowers, as well as round, heavy rocks.)

WORK PERIOD:

• The child colors the 8" X 10" rectangle, leaving no white spaces.

• The child covers the area with paint to which a few drops of liquid dish detergent has been added. (This helps the paint adhere to the waxy surface.)

• While the paint is drying, have the child sketch his drawing on a separate sheet of paper. Talk about using different thicknesses of line for different objects.

• When the paint is dry, have the child etch the drawing, using at least 3 different thicknesses of line.

QUESTIONS FOR EVALUATION AND REVIEW:

Show me where you made lines of different contour. Why did you choose those lines?

LESSON 6, YEAR A **Shape Design** **Date** ______________

BIG IDEA: Shapes can influence feelings and attitudes. (S3)

GOAL: The child will use various shapes to create a feeling in a drawing.

MAIN ELEMENT: Shape

MATERIALS: Markers
Drawing paper

STRATEGY:

• Review with your child the meaning of the word "shape". Remind your child that a shape is any form that is enclosed with one continuous line. It can have an identifiable name (such as a square or triangle) or it may have no name at all (such as a "blob").

• Brainstorm a list of words that depict feeling and write them down. Include words such as "happy", "sad", "excited", "worried", etc.

• Go over each emotion, one at a time. Ask your child to draw a shape that would describe that emotion next to its name. For example, a child might associate a lightning-bolt shape with an angry feeling, or a balloon shape with a happy feeling. (If your child has difficulty with this, it may help to have him draw different kinds of shapes first, then choose an emotion to go with each shape.)

WORK PERIOD:

• The child selects an emotion that he would like to depict.

• Discuss with your child what kinds of shape would express that feeling.

• The child uses two or more different shapes to fill the page. (NOTE: You may want to save this project for review in Lesson 13.)

QUESTIONS FOR EVALUATION AND REVIEW:

What shape(s) did you choose for your design? Why?

Does your design feel the way you wanted it to feel? Why or why not?

LESSON 7, YEAR A **Something Special** **Date** ______________

BIG IDEA: Detail can emphasize main shapes. (S2)

GOAL: The child will draw an assortment of things that are special to him, emphasizing one item which is most important by giving it more detail than the others.

MAIN ELEMENT: Shape

MATERIALS:

Drawing paper
Markers
Special possessions

STRATEGY:

- Have your child gather about five of his favorite possessions.

- Explain that sometimes artists draw or paint things that are special to them.

WORK PERIOD:

- Have the child decide on the one possession that is the most special and examine it carefully. Ask him to show you some of its details. (For example, a stuffed animal may have a label, an applique, sewn-on eyelashes, etc.)

- Child points to the place on the paper where the most special possession will go. Explain that one way to show that something is special is to give it more detail than the other objects.

- Have the child draw his special object first, adding as much detail as possible.

- The child completes the drawing by adding the other objects, which should have less detail than the special object.

QUESTIONS FOR EVALUATION AND REVIEW:

Do you see how adding detail to your _____ shows how special it is to you?

How do you feel about your drawing?

LESSON 8, YEAR A **Nature Prints** Date

BIG IDEA: Shapes occur in the environment and can be organic. (S1)

GOAL: The child will use naturally-occuring shapes in a nature print design.

MAIN ELEMENT: Shape

MATERIALS:

Assorted objects from nature (ex., leaves, rocks, sticks, sea shells, pine branches, pine cones, fruits, vegetables)
Tempera paints
Colored or large paper
Brush
Water bowl
Newspaper
Smock

STRATEGY:

• Look at the objects that have been collected. Review the difference between a **shape** and a **form**. (A shape is flat, but a form has roundness; that is, it is three-dimensional.) Point out, however, that most forms have a flat side, and that side can create a shape.

• Help your child find the flat side of each object and trace its shape with his finger. Point out that shapes are not just made by people, but can be found in nature.

• Demonstrate the printing technique. Choose an object and find its flattest side. Paint that side and press it on to the paper.

• Arrange objects on the paper to investigate different patterns that can be made. If desired, talk about the possibilities of overlapping the prints to create the impression of depth. *(See Lesson 4.)*

WORK PERIOD:

• The child decides on two or three objects to use in his print.

• The child prints with the objects. *(If the child makes a smudge, ask if it can be covered with an extra print. Point out that artists generally work their mistakes into the finished project.)* Save a sample print for use in Lesson 14.

QUESTIONS FOR EVALUATION AND REVIEW:

Where did you find these shapes? *(nature)* Are all shapes made by man? *(no)*

Tell me about your prints. What section do you like best? What makes that part special?

LESSON 9, YEAR A **Mock Stained Glass** **Date** _______________

BIG IDEA: Colors can be blended or swirled. (C4)

GOAL: The child will observe the blending of colors by making mock stained glass.

MAIN ELEMENT: Color

MATERIALS:
"King David With Harp" *(from Masterpak)* or other sample of stained glass
Old crayons or candles
Waxed paper
Vegetable peeler
Iron *(to be used ONLY with parental supervision!)*
Newspaper
Colored construction paper
Scissors
Stapler or tape

STRATEGY:

• Prepare the work area by heating the iron and placing a heavy pad of newspaper on the ironing board. Lay several sheets of newspaper over the work area to catch any wax scraps.

• Look at the stained glass sample. (If possible, look at actual samples of stained glass or visit a craft store where stained glass is made.) Point out to your child the swirled effect of the color in the glass, noting that colors do not have to be applied evenly but can be blended or swirled. Tell your child that he is going to blend colors to make his own "stained glass".

• Demonstrate the technique. Cut two pieces of waxed paper, each between five and eleven inches long. Use the vegetable peeler to scrape shavings from the crayons or candles. Allow shavings of different colors to overlap so that the colors will blend when heated. (Do not cover the waxed paper too heavily.) Place the second sheet of waxed paper on top and carefully carry the "sandwich" to the ironing board. Cover with several sheets of newspaper and press firmly with the iron. Remove the iron and the newspaper to observe the blended colors in between the layers of waxed paper.

WORK PERIOD:

• The child prepares his "stained glass" and irons it with adult assistance.

• The child cuts a frame from colored construction paper and staples or tapes his "stained glass" inside the frame. (Finished "stained glass" can be placed in a sunny window to enhance its beauty.)

QUESTIONS FOR EVALUATION AND REVIEW:

Do you see where the colors blended in your "stained glass"? Point them out to me.

LESSON 10, YEAR A **Crayon Tracing** **Date** ______________

BIG IDEA: Repeated colors can create rhythm. (C7)

GOAL: The child will create rhythm by using repetition in a crayon tracing.

MAIN ELEMENT: Color

MATERIALS:

Pictures of nature that contain repeating colors, such as water scenes or landscapes
Crayons
Paper (roughly 8" by 5")
Pencil or pen

STRATEGY:

• Look at the nature scenes and identify the repeating colors. Point out how the repeating colors create a feeling of movement, which is called **rhythm**.

• Demonstrate the crayon tracing technique. Select two or three colors of crayons. Take a piece of paper and fill it with bands (about 1" wide) of alternating colors. Color heavily over each band to fill the space completely. Place the colored side of the paper on top of a second sheet of paper. Use the pencil or pen to draw a simple picture or design on the **back** of the colored sheet of paper. When you lift off the colored paper, it will leave an impression of your design on the bottom sheet of paper.

WORK PERIOD:

• The child selects two or three colors of crayons for his tracing.

• The child plans the picture or design he will draw.

• The child fills one paper with crayon and traces his picture onto the second sheet of paper.

QUESTIONS FOR EVALUATION AND REVIEW:

What kind of rhythm does your tracing have?

How did you get the rhythm into your design? *(by repeating colors)*

How do you feel about your design?

BIG IDEA: Repeated textures can create rhythm. (T2)

GOAL: The child will create rhythm in a gadget printing design.

MAIN ELEMENT: Texture

MATERIALS:

Household gadgets with varying textures (ex., aluminum foil ball, sponge, cotton swab, corrugated cardboard, etc.)
Tempera paints
Smock
2-3 styrofoam plates
Scrap paper
Newspaper
Brush *(if desired)*
Cotton fabric of a plain color, approximately 9 inches square *(NOTE: You may choose to print with fabric paints on an article of clothing.)*
Masking tape
Cardboard

STRATEGY:

• Review the concept of rhythm from the last lesson. Remind the child that he created rhythm by using repeated colors. Tell him that he can also create a feeling of rhythm by repeating textures.

• Look at the gadgets your child has selected and determine the texture of each one.

• Demonstrate the gadget printing technique that works best for you. (You may pour a little paint on a paper plate and dip the gadget, or you may brush paint directly on to the gadget.) Practice printing the gadget on scrap paper until you get a clear print.

WORK PERIOD:

• Help your child decide on two or three gadgets of varying textures for his design.

• The child practices the printing technique on scrap paper until he can get clear prints.

• The child prepares the fabric by taping it securely to the cardboard. He then makes a specific pattern of prints across the fabric. *(Save the print for use in Lesson 14.)*

QUESTIONS FOR EVALUATION AND REVIEW:

Tell me about the pattern you made. How did you get the feeling of rhythm into it? *(by repeating textures)* How do you feel about your design?

OBJECTIVE: Lines vary, depending on tool and medium. (L53)

GOAL: The child will varying lines in an aluminum pan print..

MAIN ELEMENT: Line

MATERIALS:

"The Flight Into Egypt" *(from Masterpak)* or other print sample
Aluminum pan or piece of **heavy** aluminum foil
Pencil or pen
Colored construction paper
White paper
Scrap paper
Tempera paint
Brush
Smock
Newspaper

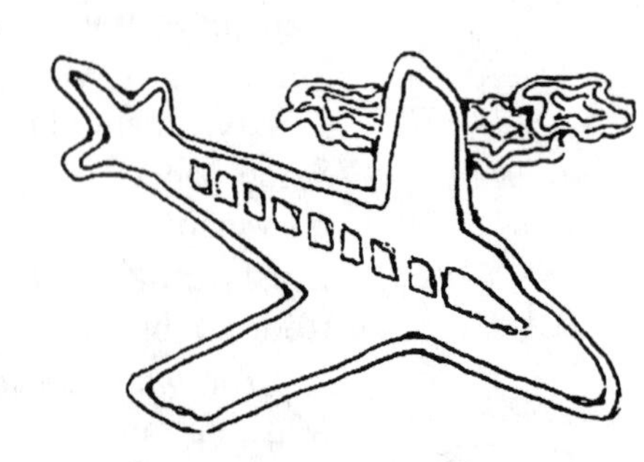

STRATEGY:

• Look at "The Flight Into Egypt" or other print sample, such as a linoleum print or wood cut. (Children's artist and author, Marcia Brown, used linoleum prints to illustrate some of her books.) As you look at the sample, point out how lines are used to create texture and detail.

• Demonstrate the print technique. Use the pencil or pen to etch a design into a flat piece of aluminum, being careful not to cut through it. Turn it over and brush paint on the raised areas. Carefully place a piece of paper on top of the painted surface and rub lightly all over with your hand. Lift the paper to "pull" the print.

WORK PERIOD:

• The child sketches his idea for a design on a piece of scrap paper, including two or three different kinds of lines. *(See page 14.)*

• The child lightly draws his design onto the aluminum, then deepens the lines with the pencil or pen.

• The child selects paint and paper colors and makes several prints. *(Save a sample print for use in Lesson 14.)*

QUESTIONS FOR EVALUATION AND REVIEW:

How do the lines of your print compare with your drawing on scrap paper? Why are they different? *(Different tools and media were used.)*

BIG IDEA: Shapes can influence feelings and attitudes. (S3)

GOAL: The child will use shapes to create a non-representational collograph.

MAIN ELEMENT: Shape

MATERIALS:

Paintbrush
Newspaper
Two or three pieces of cardboard (heavy enough to bend, but light enough to cut), no larger than 8½ by 11 inches each
Pencil
Scissors
Glue
Mod Podge® craft gloss
Smock
Samples of non-representational art, such as Mondrian's "Broadway Boogie Woogie", Vasarely's "Eridan II", or Pollock's "Autumn Rhythm" *(from the Masterpak)*

STRATEGY:

• Refer back to Lesson 6. Remind your child how he drew shapes to represent different feelings. Explain that he will be doing this again, but in a **non-representational** design. (This is a design that does not look like anything real, but is simply a design of shapes.) Look at the art samples.

• Discuss the different kinds of prints that your child has already made (nature print, gadget print, aluminum pan print). Explain that he will be making a different kind of print, using pieces of cardboard glued on to a background. This is called a **collograph**.

WORK PERIOD:

• Have your child decide on a feeling he would like to convey and the shape(s) he will use.

• Have your child save one piece of cardboard for the background. On the other(s), he should draw the shapes he wants and cut them out.

• The child then glues the shapes onto the background piece.

• The child covers the finished collograph with Mod Podge® and allows it to dry thoroughly for use in the next lesson.

QUESTIONS FOR EVALUATION AND REVIEW:

What feeling does your collograph show? How did you show it? *(by using selected shapes)*

LESSON 14, YEAR A **Collograph II** **Date** ____________

BIG IDEA: Shapes can influence feelings and attitudes. (S3)

GOAL: The child completes a collograph print to determine how the shapes influence feelings and attitudes.

MAIN ELEMENT: Shape

MATERIALS:

Collograph plate (made in previous lesson)
Paint
Brush
Paper
Newspaper
Smock
Samples of prints from previous lessons

STRATEGY:

• Gather samples of prints the child has already made in Lessons 8, 11, and 12. Review the different kinds of prints and how they were made. Explain that a collograph print is made just like the aluminum pan print.

WORK PERIOD:

• Have the child apply paint to the entire collograph, being sure to cover all of the raised shapes.

• The child carefully places a piece of paper on top of the painted surface and rubs lightly all over.

• The child lifts the paper off to "pull" the print.

• Tell your child that the collograph plate may be rinsed **lightly** with water and used again. (Your child may want to experiment by painting different shapes in different colors before printing.)

QUESTIONS FOR EVALUATION AND REVIEW:

How does the collograph print compare with the plate? Do the shapes still show the feeling you wanted?

Compare this print with the other ones you made. Which did you enjoy making the most? The least?

LESSON 15, YEAR A **Color Mixing** **Date** ______________

BIG IDEA: A color's value can be changed by adding white (tints) or black (shades). (C3)

GOAL: The child will discover and create tints and shades.

MAIN ELEMENT: Color

MATERIALS:

Tempera paint (red, yellow, blue, green, magenta, black, and white)
Brush
Water bowl
Paper
Newspaper
Smock
Paper plates for mixing paints
Charts *(See next two pages.)*

STRATEGY:

• Show the child the color charts. You or your child (or both of you) can paint in the circles as indicated. (Leave the unlabelled circles blank.) Explain that you will be finding out how to make **tints** (colors made by adding white) and **shades** (colors made by adding black).

WORK PERIOD:

• Help your child follow the "directions" on the charts to mix the new colors on paper plates. Have him paint the new color on to the first circle after the equal sign. If your child knows the name for the new color (such as pink or gray), have him write the name underneath the circle.

• To extend the lesson, have your child experiment by adding more white to a tint he has made (or more black to a shade). What happens to the tint or shade? Paint the new color in the second circle after the equal sign.

• If the child desires, allow him or her to make a painting which includes some of the "new" colors.

QUESTIONS FOR EVALUATION AND REVIEW:

Show me how you made the tints. What is a tint? *(a color plus white)*

Show me how you made the shades. What is a shade? *(a color plus black)*

TINTS

red + white =

blue + white =

yellow + white =

green + white =

black + white =

magenta + white =

SHADES

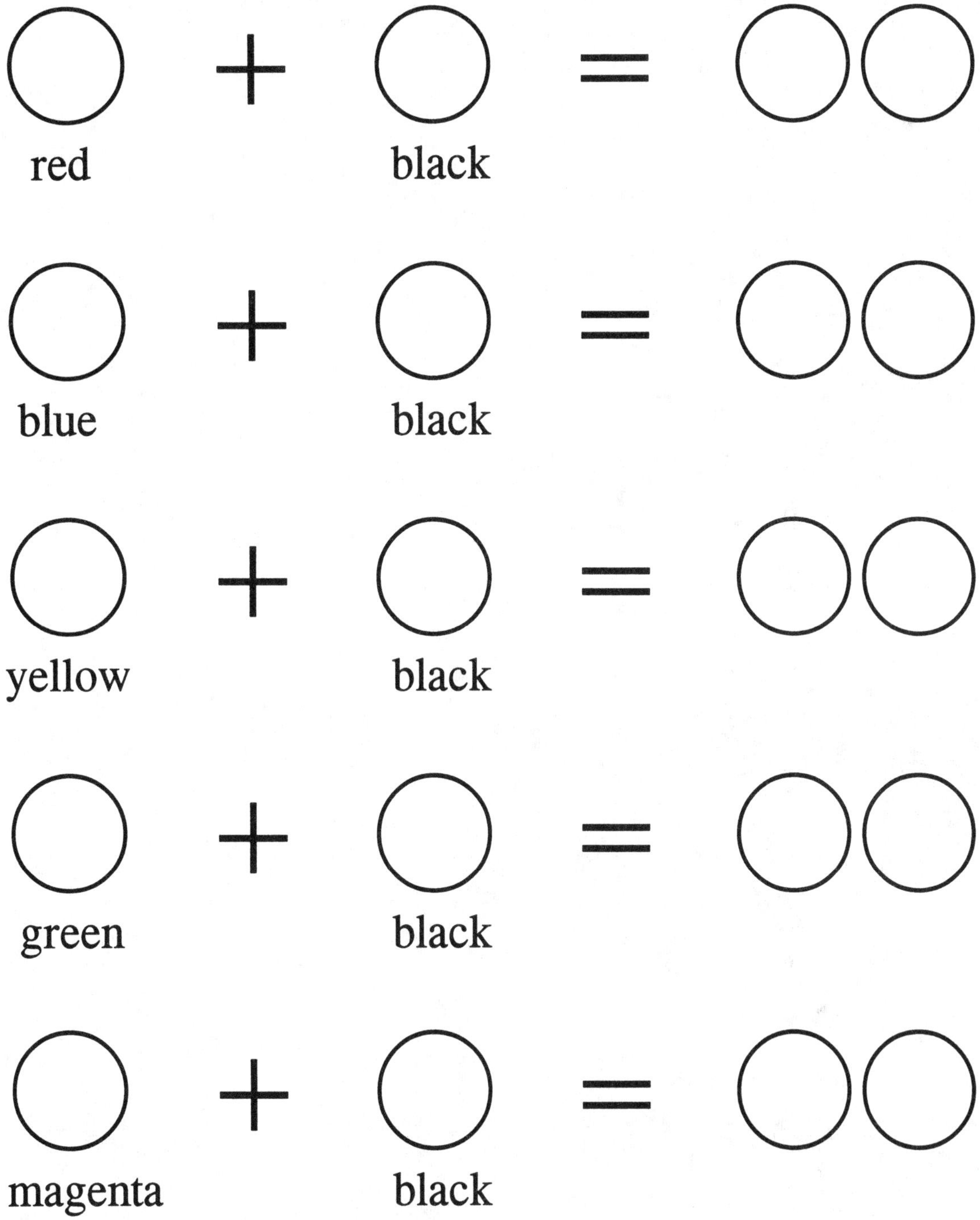

○ + ○ = ○○
red black

○ + ○ = ○○
blue black

○ + ○ = ○○
yellow black

○ + ○ = ○○
green black

○ + ○ = ○○
magenta black

LESSON 16, YEAR A **Oil Pastel Resist** **Date** ______________

BIG IDEA:
Colors can create contrast. (C6)

GOAL:
The child will use color to create contrast in an oil pastel resist painting.

MAIN ELEMENT:
Color

MATERIALS:
Black paint, thinned with water
Brush
Water bowl
Paper
Newspaper
Smock
Oil pastel crayons
Van Gogh's "Starry Night" *(from the Masterpak)* or other painting that shows contrast *(optional)*

STRATEGY:

• If possible, look at "Starry Night" and note how the bright stars seem to glow in the night sky. This is an example of **contrast**. Explain that **contrast** refers to the effect that colors have on one another. For example, when light or bright colors are placed against dark or dull ones, **contrast** makes the bright colors seem brighter and the dark colors seem darker. In this activity, the child will use light, bright colors to create a drawing, which will **contrast** with the black paint that is brushed over it.

• Demonstrate the resist technique. Draw your picture with light, bright colors, pressing hard with the pastel crayon. When finished, paint over the drawing with thin black paint, using light, quick strokes.

WORK PERIOD:

• The child decides on a particular scene that he would like to depict.

• The child chooses at least three oil pastels in light, bright colors.

• The child draws his picture, then paints over the scene, as previously demonstrated.

QUESTIONS FOR EVALUATION AND REVIEW:

What does the black paint do to the colors? *(It makes them appear lighter and brighter than they really are.)* Do you remember what this effect is called? *(contrast)*

LESSON 17, YEAR A **Non-Representational Design** **Date** ______________

BIG IDEA: Colors have complements. (C1)

GOAL: The child will use complementary colors in a non-representational design.

MAIN ELEMENT: Color

MATERIALS:

Tempera paint
Brush
Water bowl
Paper
Newspaper
Smock
Color wheel *(See next page.)*
Samples of non-representational art *(See Lesson 13.)*

- Have your child use paint to fill in the color wheel on the next page.

- Explain that the colors that are on opposite sides of the wheel are called **complementary colors** (or **complements**). Artists have found that these colors go together well. Ask your child to identify the complements (ie., green and red, violet and yellow, blue and orange).

- Look at the samples of non-representational art. Remind your child that pieces of non-representational art are not meant to look like anything; they are just designs.

WORK PERIOD:

- Help the child decide on a pair of complementary colors he would like to use.

- The child uses his colors to create a non-representational design.

QUESTIONS FOR EVALUATION AND REVIEW:

What colors did you use in your painting? Why did you choose those two? *(because they are complementary colors)*

What do we call art like this that doesn't look like anything? *(non-representational)*

COLOR WHEEL

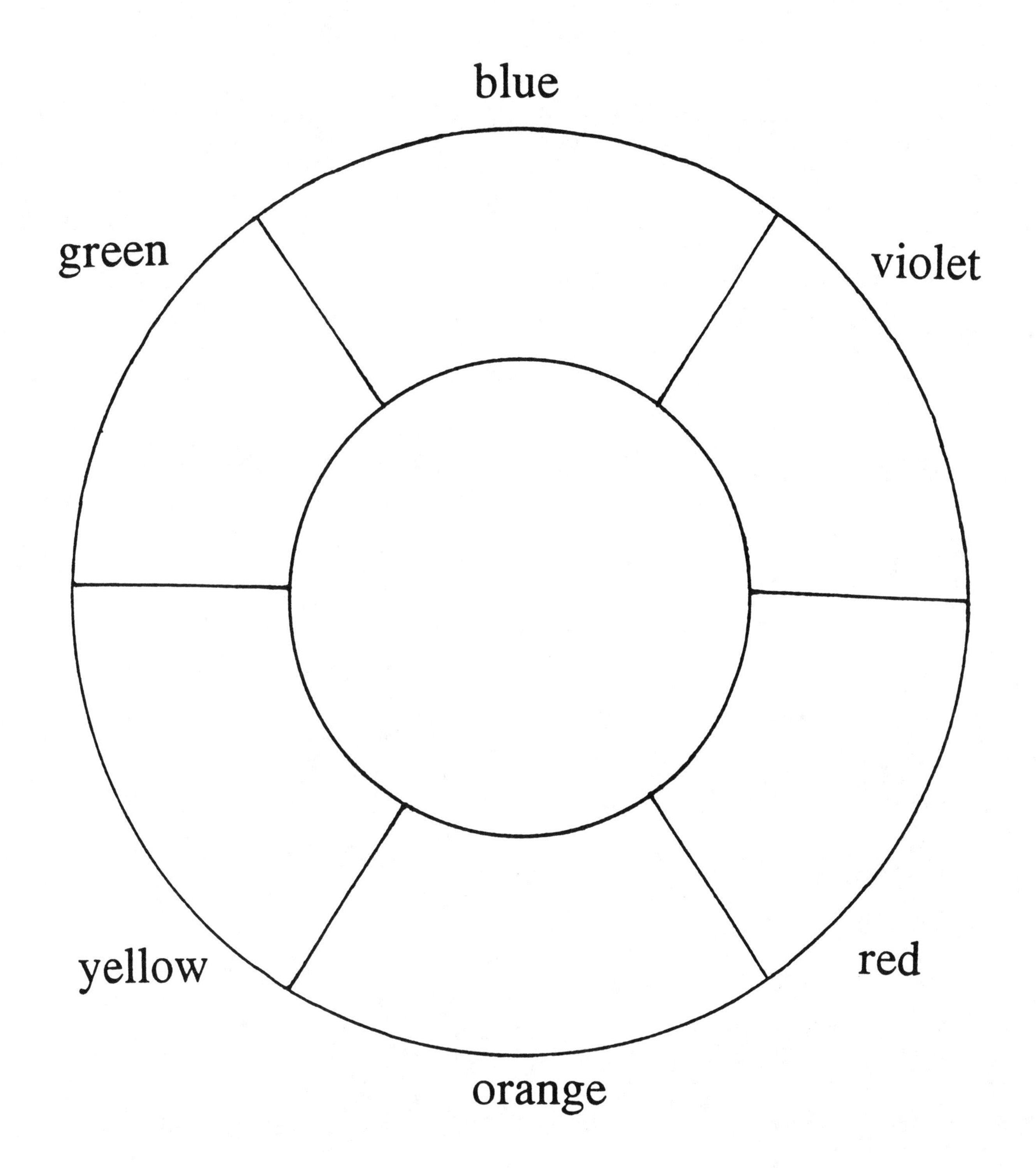

LESSON 18, YEAR A **Chalk Resist** **Date** ______________

BIG IDEA: Colors can be neutral. (C2)

GOAL: The child will use neutral colors in a chalk resist.

MAIN ELEMENT: Color

MATERIALS:

Tempera paint
Paper
Chalk (any color)
Brush
Water bowl
Styrofoam plates
Newspaper
Smock
Picture of the Bayeux Tapestry *(from the Masterpak- optional)*

STRATEGY:

• If possible, look at the picture of the Bayeux Tapestry. Explain that this tapestry was made to remember the battle in which William of Normandy defeated England. Observe the battle scenes that were stitched into the cloth in primarily **neutral** colors. **Neutral** colors are mixed, not pure colors. They are made by mixing a color with its complement.

• Experiment with the paints on the styrofoam plates to create neutral colors. Try adding green to red, blue to orange, and purple to yellow, starting with only a dab at first, then adding increasing amounts. Notice that the colors that are created are commonly called "earth tones".

WORK PERIOD:

• Have your child select a piece of chalk (any color) to outline his picture.

• The child chooses crayons that match the colors he created with paint and fills in the picture.

• When the picture is finished, the child paints the entire surface with black tempera paint. (The paint will soak into the chalk while resisting the crayon.)

QUESTIONS FOR EVALUATION AND REVIEW:

What colors did you choose for your drawing? What are these colors called? *(neutral)* How are they formed? *(by mixing colors with their complements)*

BIG IDEA: Lines have contour; they are thick or thin. (L2)

GOAL: The child will use lines of different contour in a batik painting.

MAIN ELEMENT: Line

MATERIALS:

Black tempera paint, thinned with water
Brush
Water bowl
Paper
Newspaper
Smock
Crayons
Paper towels

STRATEGY:

• Review with your child the idea of **contour**. *(See Lesson 5.)* Have your child draw two or three lines of different contour if he is still unsure of the concept.

• Explain that, in the last lesson, your child used the technique of **resist**. Tell your child that a similar technique for blocking out paint in certain areas is called **batik**.

• Demonstrate the technique. Draw a picture in crayon, applying the crayon heavily. Crinkle the paper into a tight ball. (This will cause the wax to crack.) Paint over the picture with the tempera paint. The paint will flow into the cracks in the wax. Blot the excess paint with paper towels and press the painting flat.

WORK PERIOD:

• The child draws his picture in crayons, using lines of different contour. (It is important that the page be filled with color to achieve a good effect.) When he is finished, he wads his paper into a tight ball.

• The child covers the picture with black tempera paint, blotting off the excess with paper towels.

QUESTIONS FOR EVALUATION AND REVIEW:

What kind of painting is this? *(batik)*

Show me the different kinds of lines you used in your batik painting.

How is your batik painting like your resist painting? How are they different? Which do you like better?

LESSON 20, YEAR A **Experimenting with a Variety of Paints** **Date** ______________

BIG IDEA: Textures vary, depending on medium and tool. (T1)

GOAL: The child will experiment with textures using a variety of paints.

MAIN ELEMENT: Texture

MATERIALS:
"Autumn Rhythm" or "Starry Night" *(from Masterpak- optional)*
Textured paints *(See directions in the Strategy section.)*
White tag board
Newspaper
Water bowl
Smock
Fingerpaint
Watercolor or thinned tempera paint

STRATEGY:

• If at all possible, visit an art gallery or store where actual paintings are sold. Many paintings will have a smooth, flat surface, but some will have very rough surfaces. (If an actual field trip is not possible, have your child look at "Autumn Rhythm" and try to see the texture created by the running paint. "Starry Night" also has a rough texture that your child may be able to see.) Have your child speculate as to how the different textures were formed.

• Mix your own textured paints by combining one ingredient from each of the following groups:
Pigment- food coloring, powdered herbs or spices, powdered tempera paint, fabric dye
Binder- glue, egg whites, craft gloss, liquid laundry starch
Base- cornstarch, flour, salt, dirt, sand
If desired, mix fluffy paint by combining Ivory® soap flakes with paint.

WORK PERIOD:

• The child experiments with three or more textured paints. (He can also use a brush with the fingerpaint and the water colors.) Encourage him to try different ways of applying the paint to produce different textures (ex., thin or heavy application, many or few brush strokes, etc.).

• The child creates a painting including three or more different textures. (These can be created by using different paints and/or different application techniques.) He might create a beach scene using sandy paint, or a sky scene using the fluffy paint for clouds.

QUESTIONS FOR EVALUATION AND REVIEW:

Tell me about the textures in your painting. How did you make them?

LESSON 21, YEAR A Experimenting with a Variety of Painting Tools Date ____________

BIG IDEA: Textures vary, depending on medium and tool. (T1)

GOAL: The child will explore how various painting tools can create different textures.

MAIN ELEMENT: Texture

MATERIALS:

Newspaper
Paper
Tempera paints
Water bowl
Smock
Various gadgets to use as painting tools (ex., evergreen branch, yarn, marble, toy car, sponge, cotton ball, Q-tip®, old toothbrush, leaf, fork, soda straw, feather, fabric, etc.)

STRATEGY:

• Review with the child how he made different textures last week. Explain that artists refer to the different materials that are used (in this case, paints) as the **medium**. This week he will create different textures using different **tools**.

• Have the child separate the gadgets into two groups: one for basically smooth textures, and one for basically rough textures.

• Let the child experiment with the different tools. Encourage the child to try different techniques to create different textures, such as stroking, spattering, stamping, rolling, etc.

WORK PERIOD:

• The child paints a design using at least three different textures. (These can be created by using different painting tools and/or by using different application techniques.)

QUESTIONS FOR EVALUATION AND REVIEW:

Tell me about the textures in your painting. How did you make them?

Which areas of the painting are the most interesting to you? The most fun?

BIG IDEA: Forms occur in our environment and can be organic or man-made. (F1)

GOAL: The child will create a form in clay.

MAIN ELEMENT: Form

MATERIALS:

Clay
Fork
Water bowl

STRATEGY:

• Review with your child the difference between a **form** and a **shape**. (A shape is two-dimensional, or flat, but a form is three-dimensional, or round.) Ask him to identify some forms in your house. Help him determine which are natural (ex., fruit, animals, plants) and which are man-made (ex., statues, machines).

• Review the two methods of sculpting clay.

Pinch-and-pull method- Begin with a sphere of clay. Pull out ears and a nose; pinch in to make a mouth and eyes. Do **not** break pieces off from the lump of clay.

Additive method- Start with a sphere, but do not use all the clay. From the remaining clay, shape ears, nose, and lips. Use the fork to roughen the surfaces which are to be stuck together. Add a small amount of water to your fingertips and moisten the places you have roughened. Then stick the pieces together tightly. (NOTE: If you simply try to stick pieces together without roughening and moistening, they will break off when the piece dries.)

WORK PERIOD:

• The child sculpts an object, using either the pinch-and-pull method or the additive method. (Encourage the child to turn his form as he works, since forms can be seen from all sides.)

QUESTIONS FOR EVALUATION AND REVIEW:

Explain the difference between a **shape** and a **form**. *(A shape is flat, but a form is round.)* Which of your creations is a shape? Which is a form?

Tell me about the two ways of sculpting a form. *(Pinch-and-pull method and additive method)* Which method did you use?

Why is it important to roughen clay surfaces before you try to stick them together? *(The pieces will fall off if you don't.)*

LESSON 23, YEAR A **Clay Animals I** **Date** ______

BIG IDEA: Repeated textures can create rhythm. (T2)

GOAL: The child will sculpt an animal, using textures to create rhythm.

MAIN ELEMENT: Form, texture

MATERIALS:

Clay
Gadgets for texture *(See page 9.)*
Toothpicks
Photographs of animals (from magazines, books, calendars, etc.)
Fork
Water

STRATEGY:

• If possible, precede this lesson with a trip to see live animals at a farm, zoo, pet store, or aquarium. To stimulate thinking about this lesson, note details of each animal's anatomy (such as a pig's tail or a lion's mane) and ask how your child might be able to make those details out of clay.

• Review the concept of **rhythm**. Remind the child that rhythm in art refers to the feeling of movement that is created by repeating something. Let your child know that rhythm can be created by repeating textures.

• Review the two methods of sculpting from the previous lesson.

• Experiment with ways of creating texture with clay. Try using a garlic press to make tiny strings or curls. Create parallel lines with a comb, or make "fish scales" with an unsharpened pencil. Be creative!

WORK PERIOD:

• The child chooses an animal he would like to sculpt, using a photograph as a reference. (To prepare for the next lesson, the child should select an animal that is neutral-colored.)

• The child then makes his animal, paying attention to realistic (representational) details and textures. He should particularly note areas where textures are repeated (such as fur) and attempt to create rhythm by repeating the textures. (NOTE: Toothpicks can be placed inside of legs to support them.)

QUESTIONS FOR EVALUATION AND REVIEW:

Tell me about your sculpture. What method/materials/textures did you use?

Show me where you repeated textures. Why did you do this? *(to create rhythm)*

LESSON 24, YEAR A **Clay Animals II** Date ______________

BIG IDEA: Colors can be neutral. (C2)

GOAL: The child will paint a clay animal in neutral colors.

MAIN ELEMENT: Color

MATERIALS:

Clay animal *(from last lesson)*
Tempera paints
Water bowl
Newspaper
Brush
Smock
Mod Podge® craft gloss

STRATEGY:

• Review with your child how to make neutral colors (by mixing a color with its complement). Some of these colors are brown, rust, beige, and tan.

WORK PERIOD:

• The child chooses neutral colors for his animal.

• The child then paints the animal. When the paint is dry, the entire sculpture should be coated with craft gloss to seal in the paint.

QUESTIONS FOR EVALUATION AND REVIEW:

Tell me about your sculpture. Which colors did you use? What are these colors called? *(neutral)*

How do you feel about your sculpture?

LESSON 25 & 26, YEAR A **Sculpture from Found Objects** **Date** ______________

BIG IDEA: Forms occur in the environment and can be organic or man-made. (F1)

GOAL: The child will create a non-representational sculpture using found objects.

MAIN ELEMENT: Form

MATERIALS:

Tatlin's "Monument to the Third International" *(from the Masterpak)*, or other sample of non-representational sculpture *(optional)*
Miscellaneous objects from around the house and yard (ex., egg cartons, cardboard tubes, buttons, string, lace, hardware, boxes, wood scraps, plastic caps, stones, acorns, pine cones, etc.)
Glue
Masking tape
Heavy cardboard for the base
Spray paint **or** single color of tempera paint and brush

STRATEGY:

• This is an excellent opportunity to visit a museum of modern art sculpture or view a sculpture in your community. If this is not possible, view Tatlin's example or other reproduction. Comment that these pieces are **non-representational**; that is, they are designs, not real things, like people or animals. Observe and talk about the pieces. See whether your child can identify from what the sculptures were made and whether these materials are natural or man-made.

• Have your child look at the objects he has collected. Have him identify which are natural and which are man-made. Encourage him to use his imagination and arrange the objects in different ways to get ideas for a sculpture.

WORK PERIOD:

• Week One- The child builds his sculpture on the heavy cardboard base. Objects can be attached to the base and each other by using glue. Until the glue dries, tape may be used to hold objects in place.

• Week Two- The child removes the tape and unifies his sculpture by painting it a single color.

QUESTIONS FOR EVALUATION AND REVIEW:

In our last art lesson, we made clay animals. This time we made a different kind of sculpture. What do we call sculptures that look like real things? *(representational)* What do we call sculptures that do not look like real things? *(non-representational)* Which do you like better? Why?

LESSONS 27 & 28, YEAR A **Sand and Plaster Bas Relief** **Date** ______________

BIG IDEA: Textures vary, depending on medium and tool. (T1)

GOAL: The child will create a bas relief and observe how the textures vary.

MAIN ELEMENT: Texture

MATERIALS:

Sand (slightly dampened)
Plaster of Paris
Gadgets for textures *(See page 9.)*
Water (measured according to plaster directions) in bucket
Box in which to construct sculpture (ex., gift box, shoe box)
Old toothbrush
Tempera or spray paint *(optional)*
Picture of Egyptian bas relief *(from Masterpak)* or coin *(optional)*

STRATEGY:

• Review the term **bas relief** with your child. (Pronounce "bas" to rhyme with "pa". **Bas** is French for "low"; **relief** refers to being raised from the background.) Look at the Egyptian bas relief, or look at a coin and notice how the figures "stick up" from the background.

•Show your child how to create his bas relief. Press sand into the bottom of the box to create a flat layer about an inch thick. Use the gadgets to make **large** shapes in the sand.

WORK PERIOD:

• Week One- The child makes his own sand bas relief. When he has finished, mix the plaster in the bucket according to directions. (It works best if you sift the powder into the water until the plaster begins to form an "island" on the surface. Mix thoroughly. The plaster will be creamy!) Pour the plaster onto the sand to a depth of two or three inches. Tap the sides of the box to loosen any air bubbles. Allow to harden for several days. (NOTE: Plaster can block drains. Dispose of excess plaster by putting it into a plastic bottle or can and putting the container in the trash.)

• Week Two- The child carefully removes the box and brushes the sand from the plaster with an old toothbrush. The sculpture may be painted, if desired.

QUESTIONS FOR EVALUATION AND REVIEW:

What do we call this kind of sculpture? *(bas relief)*

Look at the top of your sculpture. Now look at the bottom. How are they different? *(They have different textures.)* Why are the textures different? *(We used different media.)*

LESSON 29, YEAR A **Paper Placemat** **Date** ____________

BIG IDEA: Colors have complements. (C1)

GOAL: The child will weave a paper placemat in complementary colors.

MAIN ELEMENT: Color

MATERIALS:

8½" X 11" colored construction paper
Scissors
Pencil
Scissors
Ruler
Glue stick
Clear Contact® paper *(optional)*
Picture of Peruvian weaving *(from the Masterpak- optional)*

STRATEGY:

• If possible, look at the picture of the Peruvian weaving, or look at items that have been woven, such as rugs, clothing, baskets, etc.

• Explain that a **craft** is any art form that is useful, such as the placemat that you will be making today. Ask your child to name some other crafts. (You may want to walk through the house to identify crafts, such as rugs, pottery, etc.)

• Review complementary colors. *(See Lesson 17.)* Have your child select sheets of construction paper in complementary colors that he would like to use for his placemat.

• Have your child prepare strips of paper for the **weft** (the pieces that weave over and under). Use the ruler and pencil to mark lines ½" to 1" apart on the construction paper (one piece of each color). Have the student cut the strips apart.

• Show your child how to prepare the **warp** (the part on which the weaving is done). Fold one piece of construction paper in half. Start at the fold and cut lines toward the edge of the paper WITHOUT CUTTING ALL THE WAY THROUGH. (The lines should be the same width as the strips being used for the weft.)

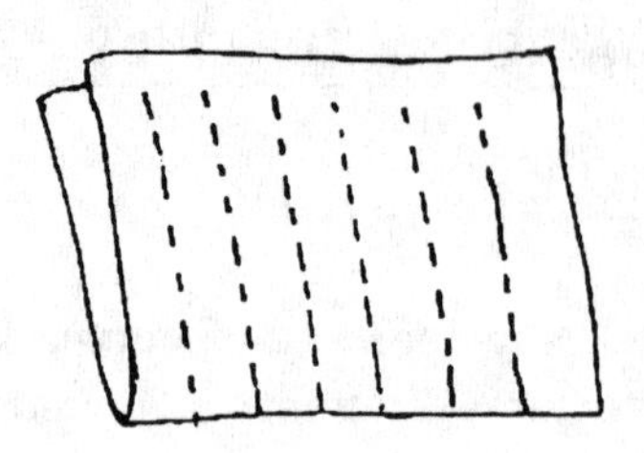

When you open the paper, you will have long slots in the warp.

• Demonstrate the weaving technique. Select a strip of paper and weave it over and under the slots that were cut in the warp. Slide the strip to the far left of the warp, cut off any protruding ends, and glue the ends of the strip onto the border of the warp. Select a second strip of the complementary color. Weave it onto the slots of the warp, but in the opposite manner as the first strip (i.e., where the first strip went **over**, the second strip goes **under**, and vice versa). Slide the second strip against the first and glue into place.

WORK PERIOD:

• The child continues weaving, alternating strips of complementary colors.

• When the placemat is finished, it may be covered with clear Contact® paper, if desired.

QUESTIONS FOR EVALUATION AND REVIEW:

How is a craft different from other art work? *(It is useful, or meant to be used.)*

Why did you choose those colors for your placemat? *(They are complements.)* What does that mean? *(They are opposites on the color wheel.)*

How do you like your placemat?

LESSON 30, YEAR A **Finger Weaving** **Date** ______________

BIG IDEA: Repeated colors can create rhythm. (C7)

GOAL: The child will repeat colors in a finger weaving to create rhythm.

MAIN ELEMENT: Color

MATERIALS: Nylon craft loops (usually sold for making potholders)

STRATEGY:

• Take a craft loop and pull on opposite ends of the loop to make it into a flat "line". Do this with several colors of loops. Have your child take the flattened "lines" and create a color pattern (ex., 1 pink, 2 blue, 1 white, 1 pink, 2 blue, 1 white, etc.).

• Look at your child's pattern and observe how the repeated colors make rhythm (or a feeling of movement). (Generally, changing colors every loop makes a "faster" feeling than changing colors less frequently.)

• Demonstrate the finger weaving technique. Place a craft loop (ex., blue) over the four fingers of your non-dominant hand. (The thumb is never used.) Twist the loop between each finger so that there is a distinctive part of the loop over each finger.

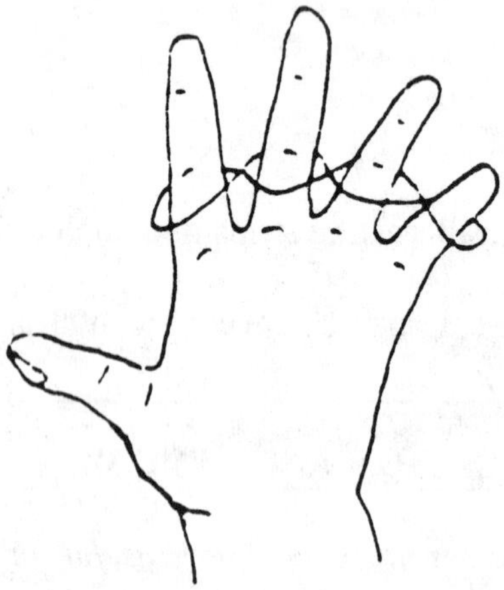

Place a second loop (ex., pink) over the four fingers in exactly the same way. Look at the **back** of your hand. On each finger, use your dominant hand to pull the **bottom** loop (ex., blue) **over** the top loop (ex., pink) and off the finger. You are now left with the second color (ex., pink) on your four fingers, and the weaving is forming under the middle two fingers. Repeat with a few more loops.

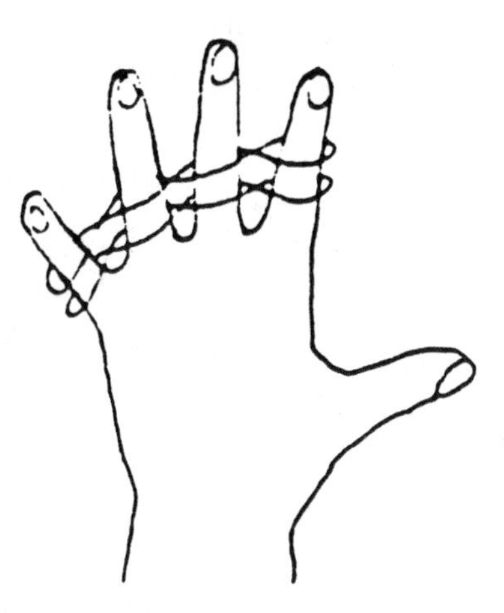

WORK PERIOD:

- The child decides on a color pattern.

- The child decides what accessory he would like to make with his finger weaving. (Because the loops stretch, about twelve loops will make a bracelet, and about thirty loops will make a headband. A longer finger-weaving could be made into a necklace or belt.)

- The child weaves the loops in the order of his pre-determined pattern to the appropriate length.

- The child finishes off the weaving by bringing the loop from the pinkie finger over the loop on the ring finger and the loop from the index finger over the loop in the middle finger. (This leaves two loops.) Slip the loop from the ring finger over the loop in the middle finger, leaving one loop. This can be slipped into the weaving at the beginning and knotted for a bracelet or headband. For a belt, find the first loop at the beginning of the weaving and pull it out. Tie this loop and the loop at the end of the weaving into a bow, like you would a shoelace.

QUESTIONS FOR EVALUATION AND REVIEW:

- Does your weaving have a feeling of rhythm? How did you create it? *(by repeating a color pattern)*

- How do you like your finger-weaving?

BIG IDEA: Repeated colors can create rhythm. (C7)

GOAL: The child will make a sand painting using color patterns to create rhythm.

MAIN ELEMENT: Color

MATERIALS:

Picture of Navajo sand painting *(from Masterpak- optional)*
Baby-food jars of colored sand *(See directions below.)*
White glue
Small bowl
Water
9" X 13" pan
Paint brush
Manila folder or tagboard
Pencil

STRATEGY:

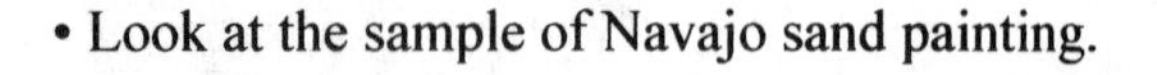

• Look at the sample of Navajo sand painting.

• Divide the sand into the jars. Add a few drops of different food coloring to each jar and shake. Leave one jar uncolored. (NOTE: Many craft stores sell sand that is already colored.)

• Mix glue and a little water in the bowl. Demonstrate the sand painting technique. Dip the brush in the glue and paint a small area of the manila folder. Shake on a bit of sand, tapping off the excess over the pan. (You can then return the excess sand to its jar.)

• Trace as large a circle as you can on the manila folder. Explain to your child that he is to make a pattern of colors. Remind the child of what he learned last week: repeating colors can create rhythm, or a feeling of movement in the design.

WORK PERIOD:

• Have the child use the pencil to draw a shape in the middle of the circle. Next, he draws two alternating shapes in a ring around the central shape, forming a pattern. Have him continue drawing rings of shapes until the circle is filled.

• The child plans a color pattern. (He may wish to make a small crayon mark in each shape to indicate its color.) Each ring of shapes should have its own color.

• The child paints all areas of the same color with glue and shakes on the sand. Repeat for each color.

QUESTIONS FOR EVALUATION AND REVIEW:

Does your sand painting create a feeling of rhythm? How did you do it? *(by repeating colors)*

LESSONS 32 & 33, YEAR A **Coil Pots** **Date** ______________

BIG IDEA: Lines can repeat and form patterns. (L4)

GOAL: The child will make a coil pot, using repeating lines to form patterns.

MAIN ELEMENT: Line

MATERIALS:

Clay
Cardboard or styrofoam plate (for supporting pot while working)
Rolling pin
Waxed paper
Cup or small bowl (for tracing base)
Tempera paints
Water bowl
Paint brush
Gadgets for making lines *(See page 9.)*
Mod Podge® craft gloss
Fork
Newspaper
Smock
Table knife
Picture of Greek vase *(from Masterpak- optional)*

STRATEGY:

• Look at the picture of the Greek vase or real ones, if possible. Remind your child that a **craft** is art that is useful.

• Experiment with different lines by using the gadgets in a lump of clay. Have your child select two lines he would like to use in his coil pot.

• Demonstrate making a coil pot. First, make the base by placing a ball of clay between two sheets of waxed paper. Place this "sandwich" on top of the cardboard support. Roll out a slab of clay about ½" thick. Place the cup or bowl on top of the slab and cut around it with the knife to make a circle. Remove the waxed paper and discard it.

• Next, take a ball of clay the size of your fist. Roll the clay into a coil, or "snake", of uniform width (about the width of your thumb). Wind it around the make a circle the same circumference as the base. Use the knife to make small cuts around the edge of the base. (This is called "scoring".) Moisten the cuts with water. Place the coil circle on top of the base and press gently into place.

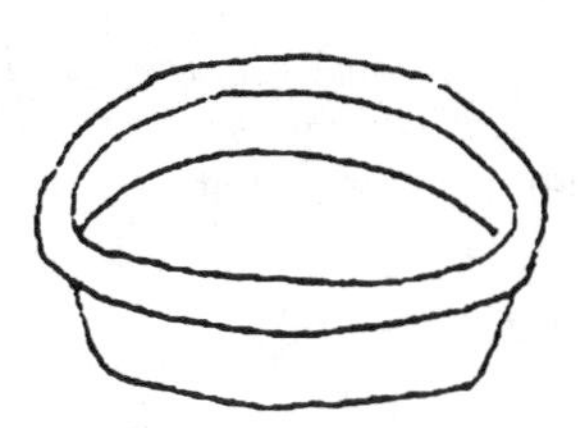

Score the top side of the coil you just made and moisten it with water.

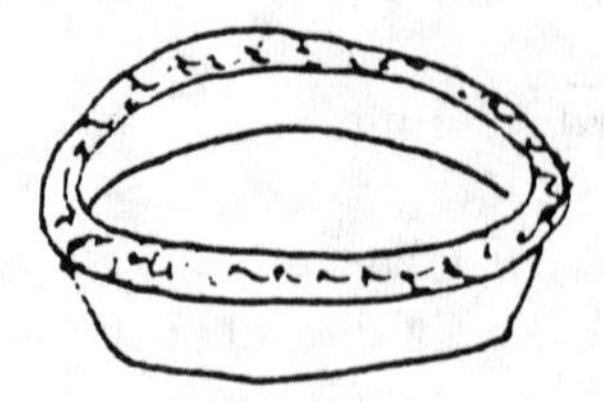

Make a second coil "doughnut" and place it on top of the first. Score the second coil and moisten it. Continue to build the sides of the pot with more coils ("like stacking doughnuts"). When the sides are the desired height, moisten your fingers and smooth out the coils, thinning and flattening them to make smooth, even sides.

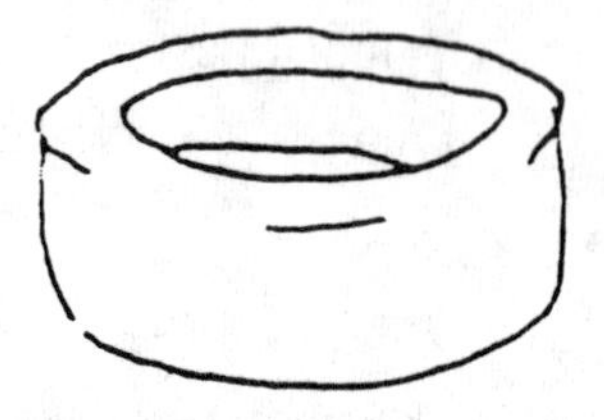

WORK PERIOD:

• Week 1- The child forms a coil pot. The child then uses gadgets to create the two lines he has chosen, alternating them around the pot. Explain that repeating the lines will create an interesting pattern.

• Week 2- The child paints the coil pot a single color. (This will emphasize the lines.) When dry, the child seals the color with craft gloss.

QUESTIONS FOR EVALUATION AND REVIEW:

What kind of pot is this? *(coil pot)*

Show me the line pattern you created on your pot.

Are the sides of your pot even in thickness?

BIG IDEA: Shapes can influence feelings and attitudes. (S3)

GOAL: The child will make a sock puppet from combined shapes, trying to convey a particular feeling.

MAIN ELEMENT: Shape

MATERIALS:

Pieces of felt
Craft glue
Rubber bands
Old tube sock
Scissors
Paper
Pencil
Decorations (such as hair, feathers, buttons, sequins, etc.) *(optional)*

STRATEGY:

• Draw a circle on the paper to represent a face. Ask your child to use different shapes to fill in the facial features (such as a heart for the mouth, a circle for the nose, half-moons for the eyes, etc.) What feeling(s) do the different shapes convey? Have your child experiment with different shapes in different faces. Which shapes make faces look funny? Sad? Happy? Point out that shapes can influence our feelings and attitudes.

WORK PERIOD:

• The child selects the kind of feeling he would like to convey with his puppet and chooses shapes to convey that feeling.

• The child makes his puppet. (First, turn the sock inside out and tie a knot in the toe. Turn the sock right-side-out. Have your child place his hand inside the sock so that his index finger is supporting the knot. Cut holes in the sides of the sock for his thumb and little finger. Put a rubber band around the "neck" of the puppet and smooth the fabric over the knot "head".)

• The child cuts his selected shapes out of felt and glues them to the puppet. (He may also want to add hair and/or decorations to the body of the puppet.)

• Develop a puppet show to perform for family and/or to videotape.

QUESTIONS FOR EVALUATION AND REVIEW:

What feeling does your puppet show? How did you make that feeling? *(shapes)*

What did you like most about making your puppet? What would you do differently?

LESSON 35, YEAR A **Wrapping Paper** **Date** _______________

BIG IDEA: Overlapping shapes can create an illusion of space. (S4)

GOAL: The child will overlap shapes to create an illusion of space in stencilled wrapping paper.

MAIN ELEMENT: Shape

MATERIALS:

Manila folder
Pencil
Scissors
2 or 3 bowls
Old sponges
2 or 3 colors of paint
Large sheets of plain paper

STRATEGY:

• At a local store, look at different designs of wrapping paper. Discuss possible subject ideas and color schemes for your child's paper.

WORK PERIOD:

• The child draws the object that will make up the design onto the manila folder. (He should use large, simple shapes, as details will not appear in this process.)

• The child cuts the design from the folder. (Since the folder around the object must remain intact, some parental assistance may be required to start the cutting.)

• The child places the folder (not the cut-out object) at the beginning of his wrapping paper. Using a sponge and a bowl with his first color of paint, the child dabs paint over the cut-out area in the middle of the folder. The child continues to move the stencil along the paper and paint, being careful not to smear what has already been stencilled.

• The child lets the first color dry, then selects a second color, sponge, and bowl. The child again stencils over the first color, overlapping shapes.

• If desired, the child repeats the process with a third color.

QUESTIONS FOR EVALUATION AND REVIEW:

Which color of shape looks closer in your design? *(the color that was painted last)* How did you create that effect? *(overlapping shapes)*

LESSON _____, YEAR A Title: ______________________________ Date _______________

BIG IDEA:

GOAL:

MAIN ELEMENT:

MATERIALS:

STRATEGY:

WORK PERIOD:

QUESTIONS FOR EVALUATION AND REVIEW:

LESSON _____, YEAR A   Title: __ ____________________________   Date ________________

BIG IDEA:

GOAL:

MAIN ELEMENT:

MATERIALS:

STRATEGY:

WORK PERIOD:

QUESTIONS FOR EVALUATION AND REVIEW:

LESSON _____, YEAR A   Title: ________________________   Date _______________

BIG IDEA:

GOAL:

MAIN ELEMENT:

MATERIALS:

STRATEGY:

WORK PERIOD:

QUESTIONS FOR EVALUATION AND REVIEW:

LESSON _____, YEAR A   Title: ________________________   Date ______________

OBJECTIVE:

GOAL:

MAIN ELEMENT:

MATERIALS:

STRATEGY:

WORK PERIOD:

QUESTIONS FOR EVALUATION AND REVIEW:

LESSON _____, YEAR A   Title: **Date _______________**

BIG IDEA:

GOAL:

MAIN ELEMENT:

MATERIALS:

STRATEGY:

WORK PERIOD:

QUESTIONS FOR EVALUATION AND REVIEW:

LESSON _____, YEAR A Title: __ ____ _ Date _______________

OBJECTIVE:

GOAL:

MAIN ELEMENT:

MATERIALS:

STRATEGY:

WORK PERIOD:

QUESTIONS FOR EVALUATION AND REVIEW:

YEAR B - PROJECTS

Unit I - Drawing

1. Still Life
2. Comic Strip I
3. Comic Strip II
4. "Bug's Eye View"
5. "Bird's Eye View"
6. Self-Portrait I
7. Self-Portrait II

Unit II - Print-Making

8. Nature Rubbings
9. Marbled Paper
10. Clay Cylinder Print
11. Eraser Stencilling
12. Collage Print
13. Line Monoprint
14. Exploring Printing

Unit III - Painting

15. Magazine Mosaic
16. Limited Palette
17. Mural I
18. Mural II
19. Squeegee Pull
20. Painting on Sandpaper
21. Eraser Paintings

Unit IV - Sculpture

22. "Fruit" Soft Sculpture
23. Rock Sculpture
24. Popcorn Carving
25. Milk Carton Animal
26. Mobile
27. Coil Pot I
28. Coil Pot II

Unit V - Crafts

29. Molas I
30. Molas II
31. Texture Mosaic I
32. Texture Mosaic II
33. Tie Dye
34. Woven Web I
35. Woven Web II

LESSON 1, YEAR B | **Still Life** | **Date** ____________

BIG IDEA: Overlapping shapes create the illusion of space. (S4)

GOAL: The child will draw a still life, overlapping shapes to create the illusion of space.

MAIN ELEMENT: Shape

MATERIALS:

Dark-colored marker (brown, blue, black, purple)
Paper
Objects for still life

STRATEGY:

Arrange a still life of objects from around the house. (The objects may be tools, toys, kitchen utensils, plants, etc.) Be sure to place some objects in front of others.

WORK PERIOD:

The child draws the still life in marker. (If the child makes a "mistake", point out that artists often turn their mistakes into part of the drawing. Help your child find a way to do this.) Encourage your child to spend a good deal of time looking at the arrangement and less time looking at the paper. You may need to assist in areas where one object is in front of the other; it will help if you encourage your child to draw what he actually **sees**, not what he knows is there.

QUESTIONS FOR EVALUATION AND REVIEW:

Show me where one object is in front of another. How did you show this in your drawing? *(by overlapping shapes)*

How is drawing with a marker different from drawing with a pencil?

How do you feel about this drawing?

LESSONS 2 & 3, YEAR B **Comic Strip** **Date** ____________

BIG IDEA: Shapes can influence feelings and attitudes. (S3)

GOAL: The child will use shape to influence feelings and attitudes in a comic strip.

MAIN ELEMENT: Shape

MATERIALS:

Large drawing paper
Pencil
Tagboard or manila folder cut into a 4" X 4" square
Section of the newspaper with comic strips

STRATEGY:

- Look at the comic strips in the newspaper, concentrating on those that tell a story.

- Talk about possible story ideas for the child's comic strip, such as going to the store, planting a garden, learning how to ride a bike or ice skate, or a trip to the moon. Talk about how stories have a beginning, a middle, and an end. Help your child determine the beginning, middle, and end of his comic-strip story, as well as the feelings associated with each part. (For example, at first the character may be frustrated, then discouraged, but shows determination and, finally, triumph.)

WORK PERIOD:

- The child decides on a picture that would best show the beginning of his story. Then he decides on how many pictures would be needed to show the middle of the story (one, two, or three frames). Have your child describe what the last frame will look like.

- Trace the 4" X 4" square on the paper as many times as are needed for the comic strip frames.

- The child draws the comic strip. (This will take at least two sessions to complete.) As he draws, encourage him to use shapes that convey a certain attitude or feeling. (ex., "How can you show that he is <u>frustrated</u>?") Look back at the newspaper strips for ideas.

QUESTIONS FOR EVALUATION AND REVIEW:

Tell me the story in your comic strip.

Do the shapes show the feelings you want?

LESSON 4, YEAR B **Landscape- "Bug's Eye View"** **Date** _______________

BIG IDEA: Details can emphasize main shapes. (S2)

GOAL: The child will emphasize an object's importance by drawing it large and detailed, like a bug would see it.

MAIN ELEMENT: Shape

MATERIALS:

Large drawing paper, taped to a piece of cardboard *
Markers
Beach towel
Magnifying glass

STRATEGY:

If the weather permits, go outside. Stretch out on the beach towel and take a "bug's eye view" of different objects, such as a tree, a bike, a swing set, etc.). Have your child use a magnifying glass and imagine how huge these things must look to a little bug. (If the weather is inclement, you can do the same thing indoors.)

WORK PERIOD:

- Have your child choose the object that will be the main idea of his drawing.

- Have your child get as close to the object as possible to draw it. (Be sure he adds the items **around** the object, too, to make a complete scene.) Encourage him to draw all of the details of the object.

QUESTIONS FOR EVALUATION AND REVIEW:

Tell me what you like about your drawing.

What part of your drawing was the hardest or most challenging for you? How did you work it out?

Which thing in your drawing seems the most important? Why? How did you show it was the most important? *(by adding details)*

* *When your child has finished his drawing, you will need to remove it from the cardboard. If you first press the tape to your clothing to pick up a little lint before taping the paper, the paper will not stick so tightly and will remove easily without tearing.*

LESSON 5, YEAR B **Landscape- "Bird's Eye View"** **Date** ____________

BIG IDEA: Repeated colors can create rhythm. (C7)

GOAL: The child will use repeated colors to create rhythm in a "bird's eye view" drawing.

MAIN ELEMENT: Color

MATERIALS:

Drawing pad (or paper taped to cardboard, as in the previous lesson)
Crayons or markers

STRATEGY:

• Go to a location where you will be able to look down from a height, such as a tall office building, a steep hill, balcony, etc. If this is not possible, have your child look down from the top of the stairs or out a bedroom window.

• Look down, and have your child notice the repeating colors. Remind your child that repeating colors create **rhythm**. (It is called this because repeating colors can sometimes give a fast or slow feeling.)

WORK PERIOD:

• Have your child choose three to five repeating colors to use in his drawing.

• The child draws the scene as he sees it, using repeating colors to show rhythm. Make sure your child does not concentrate on one or two objects but fills the page.

QUESTIONS FOR EVALUATION AND REVIEW:

How does the "bird's eye view" make your drawing more interesting?

Show me the repeating colors in your drawing.

How do you like your drawing?

LESSON 6, YEAR B **Self Portrait I** **Date** ____________

BIG IDEA: Lines can represent mass. (L1)

GOAL: The child will use lines to represent mass in a self-portrait.

MAIN ELEMENT: Line

MATERIALS:

Pencil
Drawing paper
Mirror (preferably on a stand so the child's hands will be free)

STRATEGY:

• Remind your child of the basic proportions in portrait drawing.
  Eyes are halfway from the chin to the top of the head.
  Heads are about 5 eyes wide.
  The corners of the mouth are straight down from the pupils.
  The nose is no wider than the inside corners of the eyes.
  The tops of the ears are at the same level as the eyes.
  The bottoms of the ears are at the same level as the "mustache area" of the face.

• Instruct your child that he is to draw a picture of himself, but today he will only draw a basic outline. Talk about the different kinds of line that could be used to represent different parts of the face (ex., thick lines for eyebrows, thin lines for mouth).

WORK PERIOD:

• Have the child lightly draw a large egg shape to represent his head. Have him show with his finger where the eyes should go. If the placement is correct, tell him to make two light marks where each eye should go. Do the same with ears, mouth, and nose.

• The child draws the main shapes of his face, frequently checking the mirror for guidance.

QUESTIONS FOR EVALUATION AND REVIEW:

Tell me about your portrait. What areas were easier to draw? More difficult?

LESSON 7, YEAR B **Self Portrait II** **Date** ____________

BIG IDEA: Detail can emphasize main shapes. (S2)

GOAL: The child will carefully observe and draw details within his own face.

MAIN ELEMENT: Shape

MATERIALS:

Drawing paper
Pencil
Mirror

STRATEGY:

Have your child observe the details of the face. Note lines on the lips, eyelashes, neckline of clothing, etc.

WORK PERIOD:

The child now finishes the drawing by adding details. Encourage your child to spend more time looking at the mirror than the paper, to draw what he **sees**, and not what he **thinks**. (Reliance on symbols interferes with our ability to see.) TIP: Hair is drawn more easily if seen as clumps and folds, which can be outlined; your child can add a few individual strands to show texture.

QUESTIONS FOR EVALUATION AND REVIEW:

Point out places on your child's portrait where details he has added emphasizes the shape (such as eyelashes on an eye).

How do you like your portrait?

LESSON 8, YEAR B **Nature Rubbings** **Date** ______________

BIG IDEA: Shapes occur in our environment and can be organic or man-made. (S1)

GOAL: The child will use shapes found in nature for a crayon rubbing.

MAIN ELEMENT: Shape

MATERIALS:

Items collected from nature (leaves, nuts, rocks, sticks, etc.)
One crayon (dark color)
One sheet of construction paper (lighter color)

STRATEGY:

- Collect objects from nature. The child chooses those that he thinks will make interesting rubbings.

- Remind your child of the difference between a **shape** and a **form**. (A shape is flat, while a form is round. For example, a circle is a shape, while a sphere is a form.) While the objects themselves are forms, they will create shapes when used in a crayon rubbing.

- Demonstrate the rubbing technique. Place an object rough side up on the work surface and cover with the construction paper. Feel for the object through the paper and rub the crayon over the area until a print of the object shows on the paper.

WORK PERIOD:

The child makes his own rubbing, filling the page.

QUESTIONS FOR EVALUATION AND REVIEW:

Which shape matches which object? Did the rubbing turn out the way you expected?

Which objects made better rubbings? Why?

How do you feel about your rubbing?

LESSON 9, YEAR B **Marbled Paper** **Date** ____________

BIG IDEA: Colors can be blended or swirled. (C4)

GOAL: The child will use swirled colors to create marbled paper.

MAIN ELEMENT: Color

MATERIALS:

Oil-based paints (There are special paints sold for marbling.)
Several sheets of paper
9" X 13" pan with water
Metylan® wallpaper paste
Smock
Newspaper (to protect work area)
Turpentine or mineral spirits
Drinking straws
Styrofoam egg carton

STRATEGY:

• If possible, try to visit a stationery store and find examples of marbled paper.

• Prepare the paints for marbling. Put a little of each color of oil paint in the cups of the egg carton. Thin with the turpentine or mineral spirits, using a different drinking straw for each color.

WORK PERIOD:

• The child prepares the water for marbling by filling the pan with about ½" of water. Stir in a little flour or wallpaper paste to thicken the water slightly.

• The child uses the drinking straws to put a few drops of color on top of the water. Gently swirl the color(s) with the straw to make an interesting pattern. Use the straw to burst any bubbles that may form.

• The child carefully lays a piece of paper on top of the water and gently presses on it.

• The child removes the paper from the water and observes the blending and swirling of the paint. (It may be necessary to rinse the paper to remove any traces of thickener.) Allow the paper to dry, face up.

QUESTIONS FOR EVALUATION AND REVIEW:

Tell me how you created your pattern. *(by blending and swirling the colors)*

LESSON 10, YEAR B **Clay Cylinder Print** **Date** ______________

BIG IDEA: Lines can repeat and form patterns. (L4)

GOAL: The child will use repeating lines in a clay cylinder print.

MAIN ELEMENT: Line

MATERIALS:

Empty juice can
Clay
Waxed paper
Old rolling pin
Tools for etching (pen, pencil, paper clip, nail, flat-head screwdriver, etc.)

STRATEGY:

- Take a lump of clay and place it between two sheets of waxed paper. Roll it into a flat slab. Remind your child that repeating lines can create patterns. Have your child use the etching tools to make some experimental line patterns in the clay.

WORK PERIOD:

- The child rolls a slab of clay that is wide enough to go around the juice can.

- The child etches a line pattern in the clay slab.

- The child rolls the slab around the juice can and sets it to dry. (The clay cylinder will be used for printing in Lesson 14.)

QUESTIONS FOR EVALUATION AND REVIEW:

Tell me how you made your pattern. *(by repeating lines)*

LESSON 11, YEAR B **Eraser Stencilling** **Date** ____________

BIG IDEA: Overlapping shapes can create the illusion of space. (S4)

GOAL: The child will overlap shapes to create the illusion of space in an eraser stencil.

MAIN ELEMENT: Shape

MATERIALS:

Crayons
Tagboard, manila folder, or index card
Pencil with eraser
Scissors
Small sheet of paper
Masking tape (for repairs)

STRATEGY:

• Demonstrate the technique of eraser stencilling. Cut a shape (about 2" X 2") from a piece of tagboard. Lay the shape on a piece of paper and run a crayon over the cut edges. Do **not** lift the stencil. Rub the pencil eraser over the edges of the cut-out and onto the paper, moving away from the stencil. (Think of rays coming out from the sun.) Carefully lift the stencil and look at your shape.

WORK PERIOD:

• Help your child decide on a shape for his pattern and draw the shape on the tagboard.

• The child cuts his stencil. Use tape, if needed, for any repairs.

• The child selects colors and stencils his shapes, making a pattern that fills the entire page. He should overlap some shapes, selecting a second color for the shape on top.

QUESTIONS FOR EVALUATION AND REVIEW:

Which shapes look closer? *(the ones on top)* Which ones look farther away? *(the ones on the bottom)* Are they really farther away, or do they just look that way? *(They just look that way.)*

LESSON 12, YEAR B **Collage Printing** **Date** ______________

BIG IDEA: Repeated textures can create rhythm. (T2)

GOAL: The child will use repeated textures to create rhythm in a collage printing.

MAIN ELEMENT: Texture

MATERIALS:

Arp's "Squares Arranged According to the Laws of Chance" *(from Masterpak)* or other samples of collage *(optional)*
Small items with a variety of textures (cloth, wood, screen, screw, lace, corrugated cardboard, sandpaper, foil, cork, etc.)
Craft glue
Heavy cardboard
Mod Podge® craft gloss
Paint brush
Newspaper

STRATEGY:

- Look at the collage samples. (The children's author, Leo Leonni, uses collages for illustrations in some of his books.) Explain that a **collage** is made by gluing things to a background.

- Have your child examine the different textures of the objects he has collected. Have him put items with similar textures together.

- Remind your child that repeating textures can create rhythm, or a feeling of movement.

WORK PERIOD:

- The child arranges the objects on the cardboard, repeating textures throughout the college.

- The child glues the objects to the cardboard backing.

- When the glue has dried, the child applies a coat of Mod Podge® to the finished collage. (The collage will be used again in Lesson 14.)

QUESTIONS FOR EVALUATION AND REVIEW:

Show me where you repeated textures. What does this do to your piece? *(creates rhythm)*

What do we call a design like this where objects are glued to a background? *(collage)*

Are you happy with the way your design turned out?

LESSON 13, YEAR B **Line Monoprints** **Date** ______________

BIG IDEA: Lines can repeat and form patterns. (L4)

GOAL: The child will use repeating lines to create patterns in a fingerprint monoprint.

MAIN ELEMENT: Line

MATERIALS:

Tempera paints
Styrofoam egg carton
Metylan® (or other wallpaper paste)
Newspaper
Brush
Gadgets for creating lines (plastic knife or fork, old comb, pen, pencil, pencil, straightened paper clip, etc.)
Water bowl
Cardboard, oaktag, or poster board
Smock
Pencil
Drawing paper

STRATEGY:

• Review the different types of line. *(See page 14.)* If necessary, have your child repeat different kinds of line with the pencil to remind him how repeating lines make patterns.

• Demonstrate the monoprint technique. Pour paints into the egg carton and thicken them with a bit of Metylan®. Paint an area of the cardboard and scratch a repeating line pattern in the paint, using one of the gadgets. (NOTE: Thickened paint dries quickly, so paint only small areas at a time.) Quickly place a piece of drawing paper on top of your lines. Gently pat the paper all over and pull away. (This is called "pulling a print".) Explain that this is called a **monoprint** because you can only make one copy of your design this way.

WORK PERIOD:

The child draws some line patterns with the gadgets and pulls several prints.

QUESTIONS FOR EVALUATION AND REVIEW:

How did you make this pattern? *(by repeating lines)*

Tell me about your monoprints. Which ones worked best? Which ones gave you trouble? What would you do differently?

LESSON 14, YEAR B **Exploring Printing** Date ______________

BIG IDEAS:

Lines can repeat and make patterns. (L4)
Repeated textures can create rhythm. (T2)

GOALS:

The child will use repeating lines to create a pattern in a clay cylinder print.
The child will use repeating textures to create rhythm in a collage print.

MAIN ELEMENTS: Line, texture

MATERIALS:

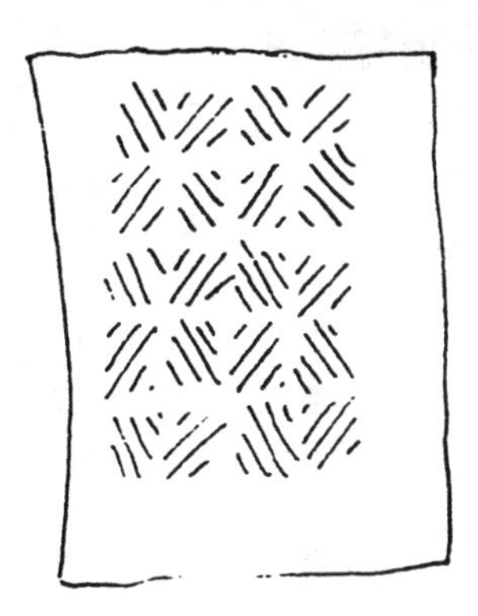

Paint
Brush
Water bowl
Paper
Newspaper
Smock
Clay cylinder (from Lesson 10)
Collage (from Lesson 12)
Ruler *(optional)*

STRATEGY:

• Ask your child questions about his projects to review the objectives from those lessons (ex., "Why did you draw these lines on your clay cylinder?"; "How did you arrange the objects on your collage?")

• Explain the printing technique for each print. (For the cylinder, the child will use his hand or ruler to hold the cylinder while applying paint to all surfaces; he will then roll the cylinder over the paper. For the collage, the child will apply paint directly to the collage, place a sheet of paper over it, pat the paper lightly, then pull the print.)

WORK PERIOD:

• The child applies paint to the cylinder and rolls it across the paper to make a print. (Let him repeat this several times with different colors, if he chooses.)

• The child applies paint to the collage and pulls a print. (Again, the child may wish to make several.)

QUESTIONS FOR EVALUATION AND REVIEW:

Show me the repeating lines on your cylinder print. Did they make the pattern you expected?

Show me the repeating textures in your collage. Does the pattern make your eyes want to move around the page?

Which technique did you like better? Why?

LESSON 15, YEAR B **Magazine Mosaic** **Date** ______________

BIG IDEA: A color's value can be changed by adding white (tints) or black (shades). (C3)

GOAL: The child will use tints and shades of a color to create a magazine mosaic.

MAIN ELEMENT: Color

MATERIALS:

Reproduction of Byzantine mosaic *(from Masterpak)* or other sample of mosaics *(optional)*
Drawing paper or tagboard
Pencil
Glue stick
Scissors
Old magazines
Newspaper
Charts of tints and shades *(See pages 31 and 33.)*

STRATEGY:

• Look at the sample of Byzantine mosaic or other example. Note that many mosaics were created in ancient Rome. Have your child identify how mosaics were made (i.e., by gluing many small pieces into a larger shape).

• Help your child identify a large shape that he would like to use to create a mosaic (such as a fruit, an animal, etc.) and what color the shape should be.

WORK PERIOD:

• The child makes a large outline of his object, filling the page.

• The child then finds magazine pictures that are tints and shades of the color of his object and cuts squares of that color (approximately 1" X 1"). For example, if the color is red, he should also cut pinks and maroons, using the charts he made previously to help.

• The child looks at the different squares and chooses those that he thinks represents the "true" color. He then identifies which are **tints** (lighter values because white has been added) and which are **shades** (darker values because black has been added). (NOTE: The colors may or may not be true tints or shades, but accept your child's answers, based on his reasoning.)

• The child glues his squares into the outline to complete the mosaic.

QUESTIONS FOR EVALUATION AND REVIEW:

Which squares in your mosaic are tints? Which are shades?

LESSON 16, YEAR B **Limited Palette** **Date** ______________

BIG IDEA: Colors can be neutral. (C2)

GOAL: The child will use neutral colors in a crayon painting.

MAIN ELEMENT: Color

MATERIALS:

Paper
Selected crayons or oil pastels
Samples of paintings done in neutral colors, such as "Malle Babbe" or "The Night Watch" *(from the Masterpak)*; many paintings from the Baroque period were done in neutral colors *(optional)*

STRATEGY:

• See whether your child remembers which colors are **neutral**. (They are colors formed by adding the complement to the color and include beige, tan, brown, etc.)

• Ask your child whether he thinks a picture done only in neutral colors would be interesting. If possible, look at samples of these paintings. Discuss how limiting a color scheme to only neutral colors can create an interesting picture or design.

• Explain that when an artist uses only certain colors in a picture, the technique is called **limited palette**. He will be using a limited palette by making a picture only in neutral colors.

WORK PERIOD:

• The child decides on a subject for a crayon drawing that he can make in neutral colors. (NOTE: The child may also choose to make a non-representational picture, or design, rather than a depiction of a real object. This is perfectly acceptable.)

• The child puts away the crayons he will not be using and completes his drawing.

QUESTIONS FOR EVALUATION AND REVIEW:

Which crayons did you choose for your drawing? Why? *(because they were neutral colors)*

What do we call this kind of drawing? *(limited palette)* Why? *(because it only uses certain colors)*

BIG IDEA: Shapes occur in our environment and can be organic or man-made. (S1)

GOAL: The child will explore organic and man-made shapes in a mural painting.

MAIN ELEMENT: Shape

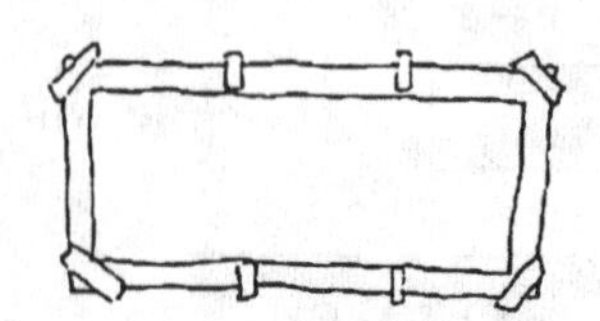

MATERIALS:

Thick paints
Brush
Water bowl
Large paper
Newspaper
Smock
Pencil
Rags or paper towels
Masking tape

STRATEGY:

• Tell the child that he will be painting a **mural**. "Mural" comes from the French word "mur", which means "wall". Therefore, a **mural** is a picture that is painted on a wall. Tape the large paper to the wall. (Lightly touching the tape to your clothing first will pick up a bit of lint and make it easier to remove the tape later.) Draw a 1" border on each side so the child can paint up to the border and not get paint on the wall.

• Help your child determine what type of scene he would like to paint in his mural. (It should be a large picture with many details, such as an historical event, a circus or park, or a cityscape.) Discuss the shapes that will be in the picture, and have him identify which are natural and which are man-made.

WORK PERIOD:

• Week One- The child chooses an idea and identifies the different shapes that will be included. Then he outlines all large objects in pencil, saving the details and textures for the actual painting session.

• Week Two- Arrange newspaper on the floor under the mural. Instruct your child to paint to the border (not to the paper's edge). Let your child paint his mural. If the paint runs, give him a rag or paper towel to blot up the excess. (Most drips can be prevented by having your child dry his brush on a rag each time he rinses out a color.)

QUESTIONS FOR EVALUATION AND REVIEW:

What is happening in your mural?

Which shapes represent natural objects? Which represent man-made objects?

LESSON 19, YEAR B **Squeegee Pull** **Date** ____________

BIG IDEA: Colors can be blended or swirled. (C4)

GOAL: The child will make blended and swirled lines in a squeegee pull painting.

MAIN ELEMENT: Color

MATERIALS:

Tempera paint
Brush
Water bowl
Several pieces of oaktag, poster board, or cardboard (about 9" X 11")
Newspaper
Smock
Several pieces of heavy cardboard (about 5" X 7")
Scissors
Comb or fork *(optional)*

STRATEGY:

- Demonstrate the squeegee painting technique. Make a squeegee by cutting a serrated edge on one long side of a piece of heavy cardboard. (You can cut a scalloped edge, a saw-toothed edge, or any design that you wish.) Use the brush to put two or three small puddles of paint (different colors) on the oaktag. Put the squeegee into the paint and pull it across the page. (NOTE: Your child may also want to use a comb or fork for a squeegee.)

- Observe with your child where the colors have blended and where they have swirled.

WORK PERIOD:

- The child cuts one or two squeegees.

- The child uses a variety of colors and fills an entire page.

QUESTIONS FOR EVALUATION AND REVIEW:

Show me where you blended colors. Show me where the colors are swirled.

How do you like the look you get with squeegee painting?

LESSON 20, YEAR B **Painting on Sandpaper** **Date** _______________

BIG IDEA: Textures vary, depending on medium and tool. (T1)

GOAL: The child will notice that texture varies when painting on sandpaper, rather than regular paper.

MAIN ELEMENT: Texture

MATERIALS:

Tempera paints
Sandpaper
Brush
Newspaper
Smock
Water bowl
Scissors

STRATEGY:

• Review with your child the concept of texture. Inform him that you can change the texture of a picture by changing the **medium** (i.e., the material you work with). In this case, he will be painting a picture on sandpaper, instead of paper.

• Help your child think of a picture he would like to paint on the sandpaper and which colors he would like to use.

WORK PERIOD:

• The child paints his picture on the sandpaper, filling the page.

• The child allows the painting to dry before removing it from the newspaper.

QUESTIONS FOR EVALUATION AND REVIEW:

How would you describe the texture of your painting?

How does the texture of a painting on sandpaper compare with the texture of a painting on regular paper?

How did you like painting on sandpaper? How is the same (or different) from painting on regular paper? Which do you like better?

LESSON 21, YEAR B | Eraser "Paintings" | Date ____________

BIG IDEA: Lines can repeat and form patterns. (L4)

GOAL: The child will use repeated lines to create a pattern in an eraser "painting".

MAIN ELEMENT: Line

MATERIALS:

Colored pencils (Dark colors will work better than light ones.)
Paper
Pencil eraser

STRATEGY:

• Review with your child the concept that repeated lines make patterns. (You may want to have your child practice making line patterns on scrap paper with the colored pencils.)

• Demonstrate the technique. Use one or more colored pencils to fill in a piece of white paper **completely**. Use the pencil eraser to "paint" repeating lines on the page. (The eraser will remove the colored pencil, leaving white lines on the page.)

WORK PERIOD:

• The child selects a line pattern he would like to make.

• The child uses the colored pencils to fill the entire page. He then uses the eraser to draw his repeating lines across the page.

QUESTIONS FOR EVALUATION AND REVIEW:

Show me the pattern you made. How did you do it? *(by repeating lines)*

What do you think of your eraser "painting"?

LESSON 22, YEAR B "Fruit" Soft Sculpture Date ____________

BIG IDEA: Colors can be affected by adjacent colors. (C6)

GOAL: The child will explore the effect of adjacent colors in "fruit" soft sculpture.

MAIN ELEMENT: Color

MATERIALS:

Felt in assorted colors (approximately 8" X 8"); two pieces of each color
Large needle
Chalk (1 white, 1 dark-colored)
Heavy thread
Scissors
Straight pins
Stuffing (cotton batting, old rags, or old nylons)
Felt *(for decorations- optional)*
Craft glue *(optional)*
Pieces of real fruit *(optional)*

STRATEGY:

• Have your child choose a color of felt. Place the two pieces that are the same color about 12" apart. Lay a darker color next to one piece of felt and a lighter color next to the other. Do the two pieces still look the same? Your child will be surprised to discover that the colors appear to be different. Point out that the colors that surround it make it appear to be lighter or darker than it is by itself. (Your child may wish to experiment further with other colors of felt to reinforce the concept.)

• Tell your child that he is going to make stuffed "fruit", just as he might make a stuffed animal or a pillow. Even though we do not often think of these items as art, they actually are sculptures. (They represent **forms**, which are not flat, but can be viewed from many sides.)

WORK PERIOD:

• Have your child choose three fruits he would like to represent and the appropriate colors of felt for each one.

• The child matches the same pieces of felt, placing one on top of the other and pinning them together. On the top layer, he lightly outlines the appropriate piece of fruit with contrasting chalk, filling the entire piece of felt. The child then pins inside of his outline and carefully cuts through both layers of felt.

• The child sews the two pieces of felt together, using a basic running stitch (-----) just inside of his outline. He should leave a two-inch opening for stuffing. (If your child finds it too difficult or frustrating to sew the fruit, he may choose to join the two pieces with craft glue.

• Have your child turn the "fruit" inside-out and lightly fill with stuffing. Sew or glue the opening closed.

• The child repeats the last three steps in making the other two "fruit" sculptures.

• If desired, the child may use pieces of felt to add decorations, such as "leaves", to his fruit sculpture. (He may want to examine pieces of real fruit to get ideas.)

• When finished, the child arranges his three sculptures in different ways to see how the color of each is affected by the colors next to it.

QUESTIONS FOR EVALUATION AND REVIEW:

• (Choose the fruit sculpture with a color of medium brightness.) What color is this "fruit" you made? How does it look when I place it next to this darker "fruit"? The lighter "fruit"? (Your child should comment on the color appearing different when placed next to others.)

• Why can we say that your "fruits" are sculptures? *(because they stand for forms, which you can see them from all sides)*

• Did you enjoy this type of project? Why or why not?

LESSON 23, YEAR B **Rock Sculpture** **Date** ______________

BIG IDEA: Colors have complements. (C1)

GOAL: The child will use complementary colors in a rock sculpture.

MAIN ELEMENT: Color

MATERIALS:

Paints
Brush
Water bowl
Newspaper
Smock
Mod Podge® craft gloss
Several large, clean, dry rocks
Craft glue

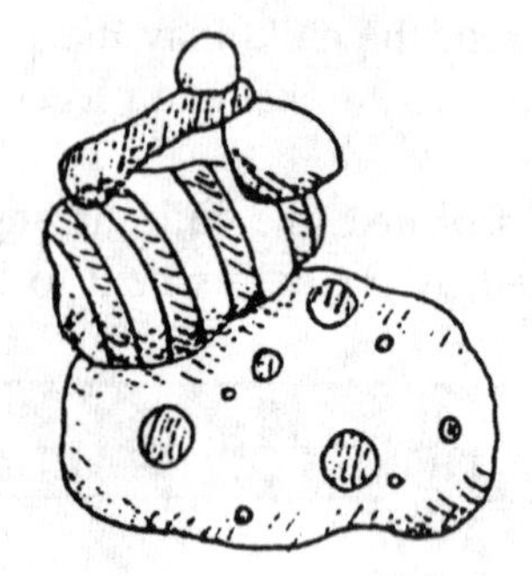

STRATEGY:

- Review with your child the concept of complementary colors. *(See Lesson 17, Year A.)*

- Have your child experiment with the rocks to find an interesting arrangement for a non-representational sculpture. (Remind your child that non-representational art is not meant to look like anything in particular.)

WORK PERIOD:

- The child selects a pair of complementary colors and three or four rocks for his sculpture.

- The child paints his rocks, using the complementary colors. (He may choose to paint each rock a different color or may make a pattern of colors on each rock.) Remind your child to paint all sides of the rocks.

- After the paint has dried, the child applies craft gloss to seal the colors.

- After the gloss has dried, the child uses craft glue to put the rocks together.

QUESTIONS FOR EVALUATION AND REVIEW:

Why did you choose those colors? *(They are complements.)*

What do we call sculptures like this that don't look like anything in particular? *(non-representational)*

LESSON 24, YEAR B **Popcorn Carving** **Date** ____________

BIG IDEA: Forms occur in the environment and can be organic or man-made. (F1)

GOAL: The child will carve a sculpture representing a form that occurs naturally in the environment.

MAIN ELEMENT: Form

MATERIALS:

Soft stone *(See directions below.)*
Empty half-gallon milk or juice carton
Carving tools (nut pick, baby spoon, table knife, etc.)
One sheet of dark construction paper
Popcorn
Magnifying glass *(optional)*

STRATEGY:

• Make the soft stone. Mix ½ cup plaster of paris and ¾ cup of vermiculite (available at a garden store or nursery). Add ½ cup of water and mix. Pour into the empty milk carton. The soft stone will be ready to carve in thirty minutes.

• Give your child a handful of popcorn. Have him spread the pieces over the dark paper and examine them under the magnifying glass. He is to choose the single piece of popcorn he finds the most interesting. Point out that popcorn is an example of a form that we can find in our environment.

WORK PERIOD:

The child digs, scrapes, and carves the soft stone to make it look like the piece of popcorn he chose. Tell him he is making a "giant piece of popcorn". Encourage your child to turn both the piece of popcorn and the soft stone as he works.

QUESTIONS FOR EVALUATION AND REVIEW:

How did you like carving? What was easy, and what was hard? Were some tools easier to use than others? Which were better for carving small pieces? Large ones?

Did you need to look carefully at the popcorn to know where to carve?

How do you feel about your giant popcorn?

LESSON 25, YEAR B **Milk Carton Animal** **Date** ____________

BIG IDEA: Shapes can influence feelings and attitudes. (S3)

GOAL: The child will use shapes to influence feelings and attitudes in a milk carton sculpture.

MAIN ELEMENT: Shape

MATERIALS:

Construction paper in various colors
Glue
Scissors
Empty milk or juice carton
Pencil (for curling, not drawing!)
Hole punch

STRATEGY:

• Explore making simple shapes with the scissors and paper. (Besides making flat shapes, your child may want to try some of the following ideas: fold a strip back and forth like an accordion, cut a circle into a strip to create a spiral, curl a strip of paper on the pencil, cut fringes, glue a cylinder, make "polka dots" or crescents with a hole punch.) Talk about the shapes individually. How does each one make you feel? (For example, a curl might create a happy feeling, or an accordion-folded paper may convey an angry feeling.)

• Discuss an animal your child might make, either with the entire milk carton or part of it. Discuss the feeling or attitude that animal conveys. (For example, a rabbit may convey a happy feeling, while a lion might convey an angry feeling.) Have your child discuss the paper shapes he could use to help convey that feeling or attitude.

WORK PERIOD:

The child creates his animal, using the milk carton as a base. He first covers the carton completely with construction paper, then adds some of the different shapes he explored.

QUESTIONS FOR EVALUATION AND REVIEW:

Tell me about the shapes you made. How did you make them?

What feeling do you get when you see your animal? Show me the shape(s) that helps give you that feeling.

LESSON 26, YEAR B **Mobile** **Date** ______________

BIG IDEA: Repeated colors can create rhythm. (C8)

GOAL: The child use repeating colors to create rhythm in a mobile.

MAIN ELEMENT: Color

MATERIALS:

Colored posterboard (two or three different colors)
Yarn or string
Scissors
Circular lid to a plastic container
Single hole punch
Picture of "Lobster Trap and Fish Tail" *(from Masterpak- optional)*

STRATEGY:

• Look at the picture from the Masterpak, or look at mobiles in a museum or baby store. Introduce the term "mobile", which means "moving" (as in "automobile"). Ask your child why he thinks this art form is called a **mobile**.

• Prepare the holding piece by cutting the center out of the plastic lid, leaving a piece looking like a large ring or hoop. Punch two holes on opposite sides of the ring and tie a piece of yarn (12" to 15") to connect the holes. (The yarn should not be taut.) Punch two more holes in the ring opposite to each other and halfway between the first set of holes. Tie another piece of yarn the same length as the first to connect these two holes. Tie a longer piece of yarn to the place where the first two pieces cross so that you can suspend the mobile from the ceiling.

• Remind your child that repeating colors can create a feeling of rhythm by causing the eye to move throughout the piece.

WORK PERIOD:

• The child chooses the colors (two or three) that he wants to use in his mobile. He then cuts shapes of these colors from the posterboard, cutting at least two of each color.

• The child punches holes in the top of each shape and attaches a piece of yarn. Have the child tie the shapes to the holding piece in different locations. Move shapes around the circle as needed to achieve balance.

QUESTIONS FOR EVALUATION AND REVIEW:

Look at your mobile. Does it have a feeling of rhythm? How did you do this? *(by repeating colors)*

Coil Pot I

Date _______________

BIG IDEA: Lines vary, depending on medium and tool. (L3)

GOAL: The child will form a coil pot, using different tools to create varying lines.

MAIN ELEMENT: Line

MATERIALS:

Self-hardening clay
Tools for etching clay (ex., nutpick, bent paper clip, ballpoint pen, nail, screw, toothpick, bobby pin, twig, screwdriver, etc.)
Newspaper
Smock
Water bowl
Fork or knife (for scoring clay)
Sample of Greek vase *(from Masterpak)* or other pottery sample *(optional)*

STRATEGY:

• Look at the sample of the Greek vase or visit a museum, art gallery, ceramics studio, craft store, or plant store to view samples of pottery.

• Let your child experiment with the different tools in the clay to see what kind of line each one makes. Have him select two or three that are the most interesting for use in his project.

• Review the technique of making a coil pot from Year A, Lesson 32.

WORK PERIOD:

• The child makes his coil pot.

• The child etches into the sides of the pot, using two or three tools to create different kinds of line.

• Let the pot dry until next week.

QUESTIONS FOR EVALUATION AND REVIEW:

What kind of pot is this? *(coil pot)*

Show me the lines on the sides of your pot. Which tool made which kind of line?

LESSON 28, YEAR B **Coil Pot II** **Date** ____________

BIG IDEA: Colors can create contrast. (C6)

GOAL: The child will use contrasting colors on a clay coil pot.

MAIN ELEMENT: Color

MATERIALS:

Paint
Mod Podge® craft gloss
Newspaper
Brush
Cotton swabs
Water bowl
Smock
Scratch paper

• Review the idea of **contrast** (such as light and dark; complementary colors also create contrast). Have your child identify contrasting colors around your home (ex., rug or floor patterns, wallpaper, fabrics, etc.).

• The child selects two contrasting colors to make a pattern on last week's coil pot. Let him experiment on the scratch paper.

WORK PERIOD:

• The child paints his coil pot in contrasting colors.

• When the paint is dry, the child applies a thin coat of craft gloss to seal the colors. (Apply the gloss inside the pot, too, to protect the clay from moisture.)

QUESTIONS FOR EVALUATION AND REVIEW:

(Wait until the craft gloss is clear and dry.)

Tell me about the colors you chose for your pot. Why did you choose those colors? *(They are contrasting colors.)*

How will you use your coil pot?

BIG IDEA: Detail can emphasize main shapes. (S2)

GOAL: The child will add details to emphasize the main shapes in a *mola*.

MAIN ELEMENT: Shape

MATERIALS:

Two pieces of felt, approximately 8" square, in colors appropriate for the subject matter *(See "Strategy" section below.)*
Two pieces of chalk (1 white, 1 dark-colored)
Scissors (sharp, but with blunt ends)
Scraps of felt in different colors
Fabric or craft glue

STRATEGY:

• Inform your child that a *mola* is a craft from Panama. A design is made by putting layers of fabric on top of one another and cutting the layers so that the colors underneath show through. Since this is difficult to do, he will be doing a project that is similar to a *mola*.

• Have your child select a basic shape for his *mola*. (This should be a shape that has many details.) He then chooses two appropriate colors for his background. (For example, if he chooses a house, he may want his colors to be red and black. If he chooses a bird, the colors may be blue and white.)

WORK PERIOD:

Week One:

• The child places the background piece on the work area and smooths it flat.

• The child uses a contrasting color of chalk to draw the main lines of his shape on the felt. (It should fit in a space about 6" square.) He then draws a second line parallel to this first one and about ½" away from it.

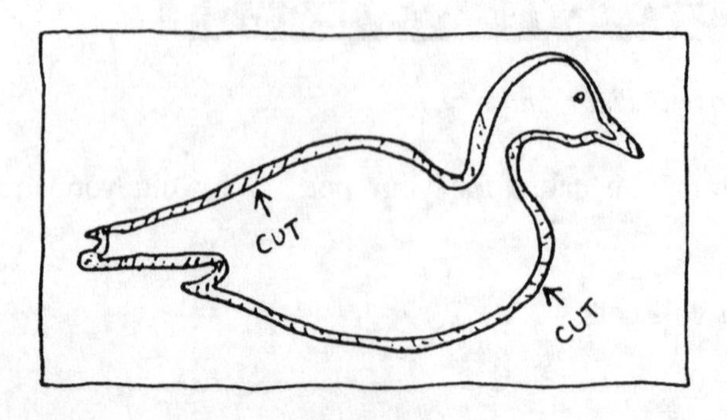

• The child then cuts on both lines. This will leave the shape and the piece that surrounds it, with a ½" space in between.

• The child carefully glues the piece that surrounds the shape onto the background, lining up the edges with the edges of the background.

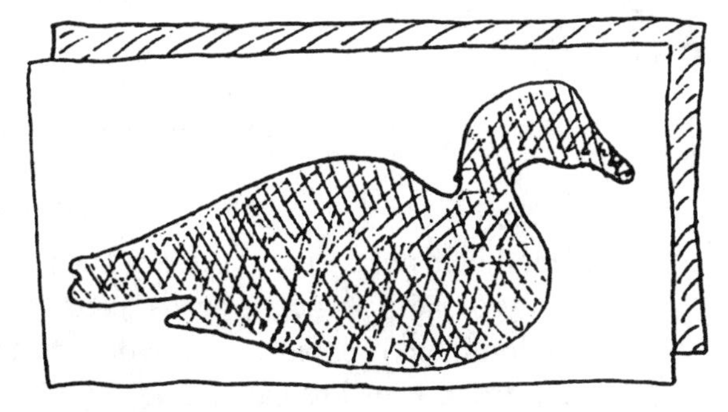

• The child then centers the shape itself inside the open area and glues it into place.

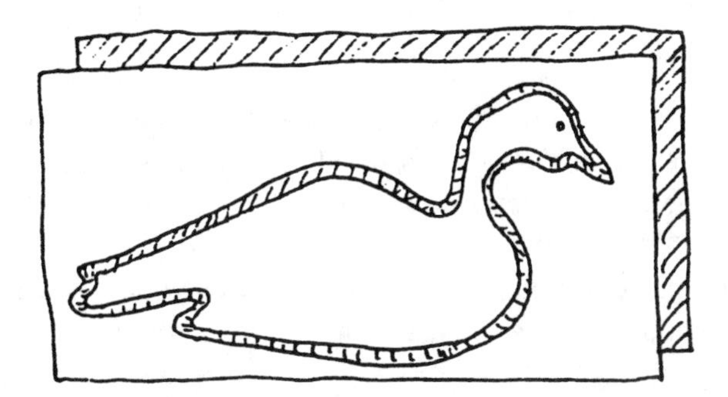

Week Two:

• The child chooses details to emphasize his main shape (such as doors and windows on a house, eyes and nose on a bear, or feathers and legs for a bird).

• The child uses the chalk to draw these details on appropriately-colored pieces of felt.

• The child cuts out the details and glues them onto the main shape.

• The finished *mola* can be placed inside a frame or attached to a dowel and hung for display. (A parent who sews could even convert the *mola* to a small pillow.)

QUESTIONS FOR EVALUATION AND REVIEW:

Where did *molas* come from? *(Panama)*

What is the main shape of your *mola*?

What details did you add to your main shape? What do they do the main shape? *(make it stand out, make you notice it)*

What would you like to do with your *mola*?

 Texture Mosaic Date ______________

BIG IDEA: Textures vary, depending on medium and tool. (T1)

GOAL: The child use items of different textures in a mosaic.

MAIN ELEMENT: Texture

MATERIALS:

Piece of cardboard, approximately 8" X 11"
Glue
Pencil
Small items of various textures, such as beans, rice, gravel, broken styrofoam "peanuts", beads, paper or fabric scraps, balls of aluminum foil, buttons, crayon bits, etc.
Pictures of Navajo sand painting and Byzantine mosaic *(from Masterpak)* or pictures of other mosaics *(optional)*

STRATEGY:

• Look at the pictures. As you look at the Navajo sand painting, remind your child of the texture of the sand painting he created in Year A, Lesson 31. As you look at the mosaics, refer back to Lesson 15 to remind your child of how they are created.

• Examine the different items you have collected. Have your child describe the texture of each. Remind your child that textures vary, depending on the medium.

• The child choose a large shape that he would like to make into a mosaic. Discuss how he could represent the different parts of the shape with the textured items. (For example, a sheep could be made of cotton balls with a button eye and black crayon bits for hooves.) He should choose at least three different textures.

WORK PERIOD:

Week One:

• The child draws the main shape on the cardboard, filling most of the area.

• The child begins to fill in the various areas by gluing in objects of different textures.

Week Two:

• The child finishes filling in the shape. (If desired, he can fill in the background or add other objects to the mosaic.)

QUESTIONS FOR EVALUATION AND REVIEW:

Show me the different textures you used in your mosaic. Why are they different? *(because they are different media; they are made from different materials.)*

LESSON 33, YEAR B **Tie Dye** **Date** ______________

BIG IDEA: Lines can repeat and form patterns. (L4)

GOAL: The child will use repeated lines to create a pattern in a tie die design.

MAIN ELEMENT: Line

MATERIALS:

Fabric dye, prepared in the washing machine according to package directions
Cotton tee shirt
Rubber bands (at least 1 dozen)
Large fabric scrap (about 12" square)
Smock

STRATEGY:

• Demonstrate the technique using the fabric scrap. First, pinch the fabric at the center and, holding it by the pinched piece, allow the rest to flow down. Twist the pinched piece slightly and wrap a rubber band around it, about a half-inch down. Add a second band about 1" below the first, and a third about 1" below the second. (You are working your way from the center to the edges of the fabric scrap.)

• Discuss the concept that repeating lines can create patterns. You are going to create repeated lines where the rubber bands are on the fabric. This will make a pattern.

• Dip the scrap into the fabric dye; remove carefully and rinse according to the package directions. Remove the rubber bands and see the pattern that has been created.

WORK PERIOD:

• The child pinches different sections of his tee shirt, wrapping rubber bands around each section. (Don't forget the sleeves!)

• The child dyes his shirt in the machine according to package directions and removes the rubber bands to view the design.

QUESTIONS FOR EVALUATION AND REVIEW:

(Wait until the shirt has been washed and dried.)

Where are the repeating lines in your tee shirt? Can you see the pattern they create?

BIG IDEA: Colors have complements. (C1)

GOAL: The child will use complementary colors in a woven "web".

MAIN ELEMENT: Color

MATERIALS:

Plastic ring from a six-pack of soda
Single hole punch
Scissors
Yarn in complementary colors (chosen by the child)
Piece of neutral-colored cardboard, slightly larger than the ring
Stapler
Sample of Peruvian weaving *(from the Masterpak)* or other samples of weaving *(optional)*

STRATEGY:

• Look at the weaving samples. (There may be some in your home– rugs, baskets, etc.)

• Review the terms **warp** and **weft** from Lesson 29, Year A. (The **warp** is the frame of the weaving, or the part on which the yarn is woven. The **weft** is the yarn or thread that is woven onto the warp.) In this project, your child will use a plastic ring for the warp and yarn for the weft.

• Review with your child the concept of complementary colors. *(See page 36.)*

WORK PERIOD:

Week One:

• The child selects the colors of yarn he would like to use in his "web".

• The child carefully uses the hole punch and makes holes along the edges of the plastic ring.

• The child attaches an end of the yarn to the plastic ring and weaves the yarn back and forth through the holes in any manner he chooses. (Remind him to leave holes open for his second color.) Ends of yarn can be secured by tying them to other pieces of yarn or to the ring itself..

Week Two: The child completes the weaving.

QUESTIONS FOR EVALUATION AND REVIEW:

Show me the colors you used. Why did you choose those particular colors? *(They are complementary.)*

Where would you like to hang this? *(NOTE: When hanging artwork, the general rule is to hang it so that the center of the piece is at the eye level of the viewer– in this case, your child.)*

LESSON _____, YEAR B   Title: __________________________   Date ________________

BIG IDEA:

GOAL:

MAIN ELEMENT:

MATERIALS:

STRATEGY:

WORK PERIOD:

QUESTIONS FOR EVALUATION AND REVIEW:

LESSON _____, YEAR A Title: ______________________ Date ______________

OBJECTIVE:

GOAL:

MAIN ELEMENT:

MATERIALS:

STRATEGY:

WORK PERIOD:

QUESTIONS FOR EVALUATION AND REVIEW:

LESSON _____, YEAR B Title: ______________________ Date ______________

BIG IDEA:

GOAL:

MAIN ELEMENT:

MATERIALS:

STRATEGY:

WORK PERIOD:

QUESTIONS FOR EVALUATION AND REVIEW:

LESSON _____, YEAR A Title: ______________________ Date ______________

OBJECTIVE:

GOAL:

MAIN ELEMENT:

MATERIALS:

STRATEGY:

WORK PERIOD:

QUESTIONS FOR EVALUATION AND REVIEW:

LESSON _____, YEAR B   Title: ________________________   Date ______________

BIG IDEA:

GOAL:

MAIN ELEMENT:

MATERIALS:

STRATEGY:

WORK PERIOD:

QUESTIONS FOR EVALUATION AND REVIEW:

LESSON _____, YEAR A Title: ______________________________ Date _______________

OBJECTIVE:

GOAL:

MAIN ELEMENT:

MATERIALS:

STRATEGY:

WORK PERIOD:

QUESTIONS FOR EVALUATION AND REVIEW:

LESSON _____, YEAR B **Title:** ___________________________ **Date** _________________

BIG IDEA:

GOAL:

MAIN ELEMENT:

MATERIALS:

STRATEGY:

WORK PERIOD:

QUESTIONS FOR EVALUATION AND REVIEW:

LESSON _____, YEAR A   Title: _________________________   Date ________________

OBJECTIVE:

GOAL:

MAIN ELEMENT:

MATERIALS:

STRATEGY:

WORK PERIOD:

QUESTIONS FOR EVALUATION AND REVIEW:

YEAR C - PROJECTS

Unit I - Drawing

1. Blind Contour Drawings
2. Modified Blind Contour
3. City Scape
4. Still Life I
5. Still Life II
6. Portrait
7. Nature Study

Unit II - Print-Making

8. Sandpaper Print
9. Kneaded Eraser Print
10. Glue Print
11. Soft Plastic Print
12. Bubble Monoprint
13. String Print
14. Exploring Printing

Unit III - Painting

15. Tissue Paper Collage
16. Painting on Wet Paper
17. Arp Collage
18. Still Life I
19. Still Life II
20. Full Body Self-Portrait I
21. Full Body Self-Portrait II

Unit IV - Sculpture

22. Animal Paper Sculpture I
23. Animal Paper Sculpture II
24. Toothpick Sculpture
25. Foil and Ink Bas Relief I
26. Foil and Ink Bas Relief II
27. Container Sculpture I
28. Container Sculpture II

Unit V - Crafts

29. Fabric Paint Wall Hanging
30. Diorama I
31. Diorama II
32. Papier Mâché Shadow Box I
33. Papier Mâché Shadow Box II
34. Mask I
35. Mask II

BIG IDEA: Lines can create shapes. (L1)

GOAL: The child will use line to represent mass in a blind contour drawing.

MAIN ELEMENTS: Line

MATERIALS:

Dark-colored marker (purple, blue, black, or brown)
White paper (the larger the better)
Interesting objects to draw (sports equipment, dolls, tools, kitchen utensils, shoes, etc.)

STRATEGY:

- Review the concept that lines can represent mass. Have your child look at the objects he has selected to draw to see the lines in the objects.

- Discuss the technique of "blind contour"-- drawing a picture while only looking at the object. (No peeking at the paper!) Explain that drawings are very interesting when made this way and that careful seeing will make your child become a better artist.

- Now actually demonstrate the technique yourself by doing a blind contour drawing of your hand. Take your time-- and don't cheat!

WORK PERIOD:

The child chooses an object to draw and does a blind contour drawing. Remind him to draw slowly and carefully, looking at the object he is drawing. Encourage him particularly to make lines to represent the mass of the object.

QUESTIONS FOR EVALUATION AND REVIEW:

(Blind contour drawings are unusual and have beautifully sensitive lines. Help your child appreciate this different look by pointing out these special qualities.)

Why did you use that particular line for your object? *(to represent the mass of the object)*

Did you need to look more carefully at the object when you were drawing this way?

Do the lines in the blind contour drawing look different from the lines you usually draw?

LESSON 2, YEAR C **Modified Blind Contour** **Date** ____________

BIG IDEA: Lines have contour. (L2)

GOAL: The child will use lines of differing contour in a modified blind contour drawing.

MAIN ELEMENT: Line

MATERIALS:

Large drawing paper
Dark marker, pen, and pencil (NOTE: Calligraphy markers would be good for experimentation.)
Interesting objects to draw

STRATEGY:

• Let your child experiment with the different types of line each drawing instrument makes. Identify the different contours (i.e., thick or thin).

• Look at the different objects your child has selected. Discuss which drawing instrument would be the most appropriate to use for different parts of each object.

• Look at last week's blind contour drawing. Discuss the idea that good drawings happen when there is careful **seeing**. This week your child will do another contour drawing, but will be allowed to glance at his paper (but only in order to determine proper placement).

WORK PERIOD:

The child draws slowly and carefully, spending almost all of the time looking at the object. Encourage your child to pay close attention to detail and change the contour of the line to represent the different parts of the object.

QUESTIONS FOR EVALUATION AND REVIEW:

How do you feel about this drawing?

Which drawing do you like better-- last week's, or this week's? Why?

Show me where you changed the contour of your line. Why did you do this?

How do you feel about drawing without looking at your paper?

LESSON 3, YEAR C **City Scape** **Date** ____________

BIG IDEA: Overlapping shapes create the illusion of space. (S4)

GOAL: The child will use overlapping shapes to create the illusion of space in a city scape drawing.

MAIN ELEMENT: Shape

MATERIALS:

Drawing paper
Dark marker
Cardboard or clipboard (to support paper)

STRATEGY:

• Find an interesting place to draw-- perhaps the downtown area, a harbor, a shopping center, a park, a row of stores or houses. (Although the title of this lesson is "City Scape", and cities have many interesting places to draw, your child can draw whatever area he lives in.)

• Help your child identify the shapes in the area he wishes to draw, such as the box shapes of buildings, the triangle shapes of sails, the round shapes of trees, etc. Help your child see how shapes in the foreground overlap shapes in the background. This is one way you can tell that the objects in the foreground are closer than those in the background.

WORK PERIOD:

• The child chooses a view that he thinks will make an exciting drawing, as well as one in which he can see overlapping shapes.

• The child draws the city scape, making large shapes that will fill the paper.

QUESTIONS FOR EVALUATION AND REVIEW:

Show me where you overlapped shapes. Which object looks closer? Which object looks farther away?

How do you like your work?

LESSON 4, YEAR C **Still Life I** **Date** ____________

BIG IDEA: Detail can emphasize main shapes. (S2)

GOAL: The child will use detail to emphasize the main shapes in a still life drawing.

MAIN ELEMENT: Shape

MATERIALS:

Drawing paper
Dark crayon
Arranged objects, placed where they will not be disturbed until the next art session

STRATEGY:

• Look through magazine pictures for samples of still life. (Pictures of people are **portraits**; outdoor views are **landscapes**; pictures of objects are **still life**.)

• Help your child arrange objects for his own still life. (Some objects that lend themselves well to still life are hats, art supplies, musical instruments, simple machines, collections, science equipment, and toys.)

WORK PERIOD:

• Have your child look at the still life. Have him look at each object in the still life to determine its basic shape (outline). Have him identify details that emphasize each shape.

• The child draws the still life, concentrating on the lines that create the shape of each object and the details that emphasize each shape. Encourage him to draw slowly (so that he can really **see**) and to make large shapes so that he can fill the page.

(NOTE: Your child may need more than one drawing session in order to include details adequately.)

QUESTIONS FOR EVALUATION AND REVIEW:

Tell me what you like about your drawing.

Show me areas where you used details to emphasize your main shapes.

LESSON 5, YEAR C **Still Life II** **Date** ____________

BIG IDEA: Colors can be affected by adjacent colors. (C5)

GOAL: The child will identify the effect of adjacent colors in a still life drawing.

MAIN ELEMENT: Color

MATERIALS:

Drawing paper
Tempera paints
Water bowl
Newspaper (to protect work area)
Brushes
Smock
Styrofoam plates or egg cartons (for color mixing)
Objects arranged into a still life (from last week)

STRATEGY:

- Choose a color and paint a square approximately 2" X 2" on a piece of paper. Paint a second square of the same color about 6" away. Choose a darker color and paint a border around the first box. Choose a lighter color and paint a border around the second square. Ask your child which square appears to be lighter. Help him to see that an adjacent dark color makes a given color appear darker, while an adjacent light color makes it appear lighter. (If your child wishes, he may continue experimenting with this concept for a short while.)

- Have your child select one object from his still life. Without removing it from the arrangement, have him mix a color of paint that he feels approximates the color of the object. Then carefully remove the object from the arrangement and view it by itself. If he notices a difference in color, point out that his perception was probably influenced by the colors of the surrounding objects in the still life. However, he should **not** mix a new color; artists "paint what they see" for a true-to-life effect.

WORK PERIOD:

The child paints each object in his still life, noting the effect of the adjacent colors.

QUESTIONS FOR EVALUATION AND REVIEW:

(Tape the finished drawing to the wall at your child's eye level.)

How do you feel about your still life drawing now?

How did you choose and make the colors for the objects in the still life?

LESSON 6, YEAR C **Portraits** **Date** ____________

BIG IDEA: Lines can represent mass. (L1)

GOAL: The child will use lines to represent mass in a portrait.

MAIN ELEMENT: Line

MATERIALS:

Crayons
Drawing paper
Photo or magazine picture of a person to draw

STRATEGY:

• Review with your child the different kinds of line *(See page 14.)* and how each kind could be used to represent different masses. (For example, thick lines could be used to represent a heavy object.)

• Look through photos or magazines for pictures of people's faces. Have your child trace the different lines in the person's face and identify how those lines represent mass (ex., thin feathery lines in a model's eyebrows).

• Have your child select a picture of a person to draw.

WORK PERIOD:

The child draws the portrait, using different lines to represent different masses in the person's face. (Encourage your child to have the portrait fill the entire page.)

QUESTIONS FOR EVALUATION AND REVIEW:

Tell me about your portrait.

What lines did you use to show the different masses in the person's face?

LESSON 7, YEAR C **Nature Study** **Date** ______________

BIG IDEA: Shapes occur in our environment and can be organic or man-made. (S1)

GOAL: The child will identify shapes and reproduce them in a nature study.

MAIN ELEMENT: Shape

MATERIALS:

Drawing paper
Crayons or markers
Plant or animal

STRATEGY:

• You may wish to plan a field trip to provide motivation for this project. Some ideas include a zoo, a farm, an aquarium, an arboretum, a garden, a pet store, a greenhouse, or a friend's home to view an unusual pet. (If a field trip is not possible, look at science magazines, encyclopedias, or library books to find pictures of interesting plants and animals.) This project may also be tied into a science project or report that is part of your child's regular studies.

• Help your child select a plant or animal he would like to draw. (NOTE: Drawing a moving animal might be too frustrating for your child. You may want to suggest switching to a more "cooperative" creature, such as a plant or tree.) Look at the creature and talk about the different shapes he can see in the object.

WORK PERIOD:

The child draws the plant or animal he has chosen, beginning with the basic shapes and then adding details.

QUESTIONS FOR EVALUATION AND REVIEW:

Tell me about your nature study.

Show me the basic shapes in your creature.

How do you like this drawing?

LESSON 8, YEAR C **Sandpaper Print** **Date** ______________

BIG IDEA: Textures vary, depending on medium and tool. (T1)

GOAL: The child will observe the effect of texture in a sandpaper print.

MAIN ELEMENT: Texture

MATERIALS:

"Sunday Afternoon on the Island of the Grand Jatte" *(from Masterpak)* or other sample of Pointillist art *(The student can also examine colored comic pages, using a magnifying glass.)*
Crayons
Two pieces of sandpaper, about 8" by 10" each
Iron *(to be used only by an adult!)*
White drawing paper
Newspaper

STRATEGY:

• If necessary, review with your child the concept of texture. Have him identify different textures around your home.

• Demonstrate the technique. Place a pad of newspaper on the ironing board while the iron is heating. Draw a picture with crayon on the sandpaper. Place a piece of white paper on the newspaper pad and place the sandpaper, face down, on top of it. Place two or three layers of newspaper over the sandpaper and press with a hot iron. Ask your child to predict how the texture of the sandpaper will affect the print of your crayon drawing. Look at the results.

• Compare your print with the Pointillist paintings. Explain that Pointillists painted their pictures with tiny dots of color, trusting that the eye would blend the dots into a complete picture. (If you are using colored cartoons, have your child examine them under a magnifying glass to observe the dots of color.) Ask your child to explain why your sandpaper print looks like Pointillist art. *(The grains of sand create the tiny dots of color.)*

WORK PERIOD:

The child colors his own sandpaper picture, which the adult prints for him.

QUESTIONS FOR EVALUATION AND REVIEW:

What was Pointillism? *(paintings made with dots of color)* Does your sandpaper print look like a Pointillist painting?

How do you feel about your sandpaper print?

Kneaded Eraser Print

Date ______________

BIG IDEA: Colors can be neutral. (C2)

GOAL: The child will use neutral colors in a kneaded eraser print.

MAIN ELEMENT: Color

MATERIALS:

Paints in neutral colors
Paintbrush
Paper *(Colored paper- especially brown- will create an interesting effect.)*
Smock
Newspaper (to protect work area)

STRATEGY:

- Review with your child the neutral colors. *(See Lesson 18, Year A.)*

- Allow your child to experiment with the kneaded eraser, making different shapes.

- Demonstrate the technique. Make an interesting shape with the kneaded eraser, then lightly brush on paint of a neutral color. Touch the eraser to a piece of paper to create the print.

- Allow your child to experiment on a piece of scrap paper until he is able to use just enough paint and just enough pressure to make a clear print.

WORK PERIOD:

- The child selects a background color and two or three neutral colors of paint.

- The child fills the page with interesting prints.

- If desired, the child can make several more pages of prints, using different color schemes.

QUESTIONS FOR EVALUATION AND REVIEW:

Which eraser prints do you like best? Why?

Which color schemes do you like best? Why?

Which color(s) did you use for printing? What do we call these colors? *(neutral)*

BIG IDEA: Lines have contour; they are thick or thin. (L2)

GOAL: The child will use lines of varying contour in a glue print.

MAIN ELEMENT: Line

MATERIALS:

Cardboard square, about 6" X 6"
Pencil
Liquid glue
Paintbrush
Craft gloss

STRATEGY:

• Draw a sample design on cardboard and squeeze glue over the lines; this will create raised lines, some thick and some thin. Let dry. (NOTE: If the lines don't seem raised enough, go over them with more glue.) Cover with craft gloss and let dry.

• Review the concept of **contour**. Your child should be able to tell you that **contour** refers to the thickness of a line.

• Explain to your child how you made your printing **plate**. In a few more weeks, you will show how it can be used to make several copies of the same thing.

WORK PERIOD:

• The child chooses three different line of contour to include in his design. (The design may be representational or non-representational.)

• The child applies glue to the lines of the design, then allows the glue to dry thoroughly.

• The child touches up the plate with additional glue, then applies craft gloss when completely dry.

QUESTIONS FOR EVALUATION AND REVIEW:

Show me where your lines changed contour.

What do you think the finished prints will look like?

(NOTE: The plates in this and the next few lessons can be printed as they are made with the prints saved for Lesson 14, or they can be saved and printed all at once.)

Soft Plastic Prints

Date ______________

BIG IDEA: Lines vary, depending on tool and medium. (L3)

GOAL: The child will use various tools to create lines in a soft plastic print.

MAIN ELEMENT: Line

MATERIALS:

Two pieces of soft plastic, approximately 6" X 6" (These can be found food packages, such as bacon, or purchased at a craft store.)
Items that can be used to etch lines into the plastic (such as bobby pin, ballpoint pen, chopstick, screwdriver, pencil, knitting needle, plastic knife or fork, etc.)
Black marker and pencil
Scrap paper

STRATEGY:

- Have your child draw lines with the marker and pencil on the scrap paper. Ask your child why the lines are different. (The marker is thicker than the pencil; they are made of different materials.) Point out that different tools create different lines.

- Demonstrate how to create the printing plate. Use the pencil to draw a design on a sheet of soft plastic. (NOTE: The final print will be backward from your drawing.) Use the different tools to trace over the lines of your design, creating raised lines on the back of the plastic. (The raised side will become the printing surface.) Explain that you will print this plate along with your glue plate in a few weeks.

- Examine the raised lines with your child to determine what kind of line is made by each tool.

WORK PERIOD:

- Have the child select three different tools that he would like to use.

- The child draws his design on the back of his plate.

- The child etches the lines of his design, using the tools he has chosen.

QUESTIONS FOR EVALUATION AND REVIEW:

How did you create the different lines in the plastic? *(by using different tools)*

How do you feel about your print?

LESSON 12, YEAR C **Bubble Prints** **Date** ______________

BIG IDEA: Colors have complements. (C1)

GOAL: The child will use complementary colors in a bubble print design.

MAIN ELEMENT: Color

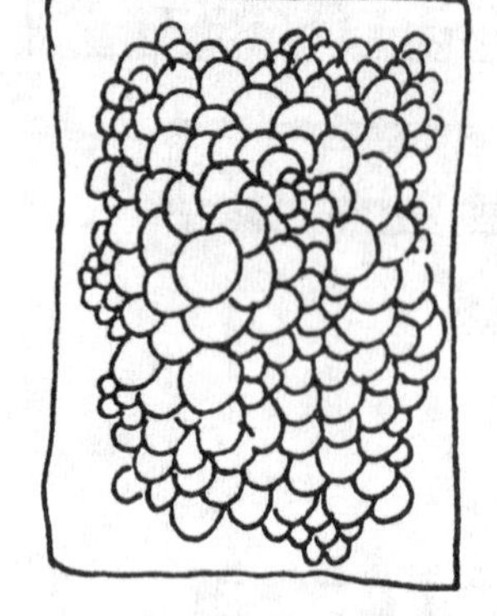

MATERIALS:

Paint
Liquid dish soap
White paper, approximately 8" X 8"
Smock
Newspaper
Drinking straw
Two baking pans, 9" X 13"

STRATEGY:

• Review the concept of complementary colors. Your child should be able to tell you that complementary colors are opposite on the color wheel; they are red and green, blue and orange, and purple and yellow.

• Look at the two printing plates your child has already made. Explain that prints will be made by applying paint directly to the plates and making several prints. Today you will be making a different kind of print. It is called a **monoprint** because it can only be made once.

• Demonstrate the technique. Pour paint into the baking pan. Add a few drops of liquid dish soap and stir with the drinking straw. Gently blow through the straw to create bubbles in the paint. Quickly place a piece of paper on top of the bubbles and lift to view the print made by the bubbles.

WORK PERIOD:

• The child experiments with the bubble print method on several sheets of paper.

• Have the child choose a pair of complementary colors to use in a bubble print. He then prepares the pans of paint, one color in each pan.

• The child makes a bubble print with his first color, then prints it again with the second color.

QUESTIONS FOR EVALUATION AND REVIEW:

Which colors did you choose? Why? *(They are complementary.)*

How do you feel about your results?

LESSON 13, YEAR C **String Prints** **Date** ____________

BIG IDEA: Lines can represent mass. (L1)

GOAL: The child will use line to represent mass in a string print.

MAIN ELEMENT: Line

MATERIALS:

String or yarn of at least three different thicknesses
Liquid glue
Pencil
Piece of heavy cardboard (approximately 8" square)
Craft gloss
Brush

STRATEGY:

• Review with your child the different kinds of line (p. 14) and how they can be used to represent the mass of different objects.

• Have your child decide what kind of object each thickness of string could represent and how they could be incorporated into the same scene. (For example, the thickest string could represent a heavy, round snowman, while the thinnest string could represent the sticks that make up his arms.)

WORK PERIOD:

• The child lightly draws his scene with pencil on the cardboard. Encourage him to use large shapes and avoid many details, which may not come out on this kind of print.

• The child goes over his lines with liquid glue and lays the appropriate thickness of string on top of the glue.

• When the glue has thoroughly dried, the child applies a coat of craft gloss to the entire printing plate. Tell your child that he will be printing with all of the plates he has made in the next session.

QUESTIONS FOR EVALUATION AND REVIEW:

Show me the different strings you used in your print. Why did you place them where you did?
(The child should make some reference to the thickness of yarn representing the mass of the shape.)

LESSON 14, YEAR C **Exploring Printing** **Date** ______________

BIG IDEA: Lines vary, depending on tool and medium. (L3)

GOAL: The child will notice the variations of line formed by different types of prints.

MAIN ELEMENT: Line

MATERIALS:

Medium-size white paper
Paints
Paintbrushes
Newspaper
Smock
Previously-made printing plates from Lessons 10, 11, and 13

STRATEGY:

• Review with your child how he made each of the three printing plates. Tell him that today he will see how the different kinds of line are created by using different tools and media.

• Demonstrate the technique. Use the paintbrush to apply a thin layer of paint to the raised areas on one of the printing plates. Lay a sheet of white paper on top of the plate. Lightly rub over the back of the white paper to make sure all of the raised lines on the plate come into contact with the paper. Carefully remove the paper by lifting at one corner.

WORK PERIOD:

The child experiments with printing from all of the plates he has made. He may wish to wash the plates off carefully and repeat his prints, using different colors; he may also wish to apply different colors to different areas of the same plate to create a multi-colored print.

QUESTIONS FOR EVALUATION AND REVIEW:

What kind of line did each printing plate make?

Which print do you like best? Why?

LESSON 15, YEAR C **Tissue Paper Collage** **Date** ______________

OBJECTIVE: Colors can be blended or swirled. (C4)

GOAL: The child will blend colors in a tissue paper collage.

MAIN ELEMENT: Color

MATERIALS:

"Squares Arranged According to the Law of Chance" *(from Masterpak)* or other collage sample *(optional)*
Colored tissue paper
White posterboard, approximately 8" X 11"
Scissors
Bowl with equal amounts of liquid glue and water (about ¼ c. each)
Black crayon or marker

STRATEGY:

• Review with your child warm colors (yellow, orange, red) and cool colors (green, blue, purple).

• Help your child plan a project with a warm background and a cool foreground. (For example, he might place cool-colored mountains or flowers on a warm-colored background.)

• Look at the collage samples to review this type of artwork and how it is created. Inform the child that today he will be making a collage with cut pieces of tissue paper.

WORK PERIOD:

• The child decides on two or more warm colors for his background and cuts out pieces of tissue paper in those colors. He then overlaps the pieces of colored tissue paper to cover the posterboard. Next, he carefully brushes over the pieces with the diluted glue. The tissue paper will not only stick to the paper, but the colors will also "bleed", creating an interesting effect as the colors blend.

• While the background is drying, the child chooses colors for his foreground objects and cuts colored pieces of tissue paper for them.

• When the background is dry, the child uses the marker to outline the shapes for his objects.

QUESTIONS FOR EVALUATION AND REVIEW:

What happened to the colors when you covered the tissue paper with glue? *(They blended.)*

Did the colors turn out the way you expected? How do you like your project?

LESSON 16, YEAR C **Painting on Wet Paper** **Date** ______________

BIG IDEA: A color's value can be changed by adding white (tints) or black (shades). C3)

GOAL: The child create tints and shades in a painting on wet paper.

MAIN ELEMENT: Color

MATERIALS:

Fingerpainting paper (or freezer paper)
Paints
Fine-tipped brush
Bowl of water
Sponge
Newspaper
Smock
Styrofoam plates or egg carton (for mixing colors)
Samples of monochromatic paintings, such as Georgia O'Keefe's "Black Iris" *(from the Masterpak)*

• Review with your child the concepts of **tints** and **shades** from Year A, Lesson 15.

• Look at the painting samples. Explain that these are called **monochromatic** because they are painted in tints and shades of a single color. Help your child identify the basic color and the different places where tints and shades were used.

• Demonstrate the technique. Use the sponge to dampen the surface of the fingerpainting paper. Quickly paint a few simple shapes on the paper. Point out how the lines blur on the wet paper.

• Help your child decide on a subject for a monochromatic painting. (Since the paint will blur, the subject should not have many significant details.)

WORK PERIOD:

• The child mixes the tints and shades he will need for his painting.

• The child experiments with painting on the wet paper before beginning his project.

• The child paints his picture.

QUESTIONS FOR EVALUATION AND REVIEW:

What color did you use for your painting? Show me the different tints and shades you used.

LESSON 17, YEAR C **Arp Collage** **Date** ______________

BIG IDEA: Repeated colors can create rhythm. (C7)

GOAL: The child will repeat colors to create rhythm in an Arp-style collage.

MAIN ELEMENT: Color

MATERIALS:

Colored construction paper
White drawing paper
Glue
Sample of Hans (Jean) Arp's collages
("Squares Arranged According to the Law of Chance" is in the Masterpak.)

STRATEGY:

• Review with your child the concept of rhythm. Remind him that rhythm is a feeling of movement found in a work of art.

• Look at the samples of Arp's collages. Explain to your child that Arp invented a new kind of collage. He would tear colored paper into shapes and drop them on a piece of paper. He then glued the shapes into place wherever they fell (although he often rearranged them a bit first). Explain to your child that he will have the opportunity to try this kind of collage today.

WORK PERIOD:

• The child chooses three different colors of construction paper and one shape for those pieces.

• The child tears the construction paper into pieces of the same basic shape and size.

• The child places the piece of white paper on the floor. While standing over the paper, he drops the colored shapes onto the paper.

• The child rearranges pieces, if desired, then glues them onto the paper.

QUESTIONS FOR EVALUATION AND REVIEW:

Who invented this kind of collage? *(Arp)*

Find the repeating colors in your collage. Describe the rhythm (feeling of movement) they give.

Did you enjoy making this project? Why or why not?

BIG IDEA: Detail can emphasize main shapes. (S2)

GOAL: The child will use detail to emphasize the main shapes in a still life painting.

MAIN ELEMENT: Shape

MATERIALS:

Large paper
Tempera paints
Water bowl
Smock
Newspaper
Easel *(optional)*
Objects to arrange in a still life (ex. flowers in a vase, fruit in a bowl, toys, stuffed animals, models, sports equipment)
Sample still life paintings

STRATEGY:

Look at the sample still life paintings. If there are several objects in the still life, how does the artist show which object is the most important? Point out the samples where the artist used details to show which object(s) is/are the most important. If there is only one object, point out the details that the artist used. Explain that often the artist will use details to show how important an object is.

WORK PERIOD:

• The child chooses an object for his still life painting and places it in the position he chooses near the painting area. (He may arrange other objects around it, if he desires.)

• The child paints the object, adding details. (Encourage him to paint the surrounding objects with less detail.)

QUESTIONS FOR EVALUATION AND REVIEW:

Tell me about your still-life painting.

Which object is the most important in the painting? How did you show this? *(by adding detail)*

What do you like about your work today?

LESSON 19, YEAR C | Still Life II | Date ____________

BIG IDEA: Colors can create contrast. (C6)

GOAL: The child will use contrasting colors in a still life painting.

MAIN ELEMENT: Color

MATERIALS:

Tempera paints
Brushes
Water bowl
Large paper
Newspaper
Smock
Easel *(optional)*
Grouping of toys to paint

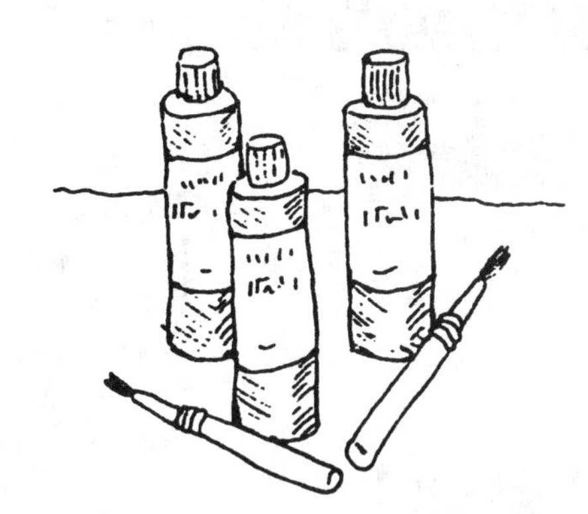

STRATEGY:

- Review with your child the concept of contrasting colors (ex., light and dark, complementary).

- Have your child look at each of the toys and describe its color. Discuss possible ways of arranging the toys to highlight the contrasting colors.

WORK PERIOD:

- The child selects three or four toys and arranges them into a still life, placing those of contrasting color next to each other.

- The child paints his still life, emphasizing the contrasting colors.

QUESTIONS FOR EVALUATION AND REVIEW:

Why did you arrange the objects the way you did? *(to show contrasting colors)*

How did you show the contrasting colors?

How do you like your still life?

LESSONS 20 & 21, YEAR C **Full Body Self-Portrait** **Date** ______________

BIG IDEA: Shapes occur in our environment and can be organic or man-made. (S1)

GOAL: The child will show the shapes that appear in a full body self-portrait.

MAIN ELEMENT: Shape

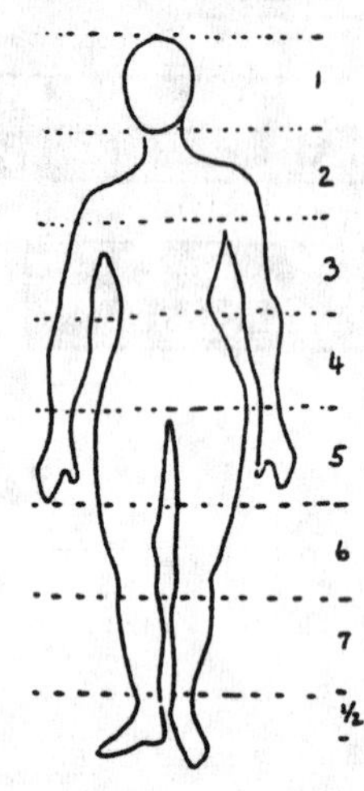

MATERIALS:

Paints
Large paper
Newspaper
Smock
Water bowl
Full-length mirror
Polaroid camera *(optional)*

STRATEGY:

• If possible, take the child's picture with the camera. (If not, study the child's reflection in the mirror.) Notice the different shapes that appear in the picture. Identify which are natural (such as the shape of an eye or foot) and which are man-made (such as the shape of a pocket or shoe).

• Tape the child's picture where he can see it, or have him work near the mirror where he can pose for his portrait.

WORK PERIOD:

The child paints his self-portrait, using the photo or mirror as a guide. (To make flesh-color paint, mix white, a little orange, and a dab of blue.) Encourage him to concentrate on the shapes he is seeing. Also encourage him to work out some of the basic proportions of the human body; for example, children are usually six or seven times as tall as their head, the elbows fall at the same location as the waist, and the hands fall at the same location as the thighs. Also, a foot is half the length of the leg from knee to ankle, and a hand is half the length of the arm from wrist to elbow. (See the illustration above.) The child will probably need two sessions to complete the portrait. However, if he completes it in one session, he can use the second session to do another portrait.

QUESTIONS FOR EVALUATION AND REVIEW:

Show me some of the shapes you used in your self-portrait. Which are natural? Which are man-made?

How do you like your self-portrait?

BIG IDEA: Forms occur in our environment and can be organic or man-made. (F1)

GOAL: The child will observe that forms occur naturally while constructing a paper animal sculpture.

MAIN ELEMENT: Form

MATERIALS:

Newspaper, old nylon hose, or cotton (for stuffing the sculpture)
Paper grocery bag
Colored construction paper
Scissors
Glue
Stapler
Pictures of animals
Markers or crayons

STRATEGY:

• Look at pictures of animals. Remind your child that real animals are **forms** that God has placed in the world around us.

• Tell your child that he will be making a stuffed paper sculpture of a real animal. The paper bag will be used for the basic form of the animal, and details will be added with colored construction paper.

WORK PERIOD:

• The child traces the outline of the animal he would like to make onto the paper bag, making it as large as possible. He then cuts out the animal, cutting through both layers of the paper bag.

• The child decides how he will depict the different details of the animal. (For example, he may cut paper circles for eyes or cut a spiral of pink paper for a pig's tail. You can refer to Year B, Lesson 25 for more ideas.)

• The child creates the details for the animal and glues or staples them into place. (This will probably take two sessions.) Remind the child to do both sides of the animal, as it is a form.

• After the glue has dried, the child staples the two pieces of the animal together, leaving an opening. The child inserts stuffing into this opening to round out his sculpture, then staples the opening closed.

QUESTIONS FOR EVALUATION AND REVIEW:

What do we call something that can be viewed from all sides? *(a form)*

LESSON 24, YEAR C **Toothpick Sculpture** **Date** ______________

BIG IDEA: Lines can represent mass. (L1)

GOAL: The child will use lines to represent mass in a toothpick sculpture.

MAIN ELEMENT: Line

MATERIALS:

Dried peas (covered with water and soaked overnight)
Toothpicks

STRATEGY:

• Tell your child that you are going to experiment with a different kind of sculpture. Insert twelve toothpicks into eight peas to create a cube. Ask your child what you have created. *(a cube)* Is it a real cube? *(no)* Why not? *(because it isn't solid; it has space inside)* Tell your child that the lines formed by the toothpicks are representing the mass of the cube.

• Brainstorm with your child different things he could represent with a toothpick sculpture.

WORK PERIOD:

• The child selects an object that he would like to represent with a toothpick sculpture.

• The child inserts toothpicks into peas to create the sculpture. (NOTE: Once the peas have dried, it will be impossible to add on to the sculpture. Therefore, the sculpture must be built all at once.)

• The child sets the sculpture aside to dry. The peas will dry and shrink, holding the sculpture together.

QUESTIONS FOR EVALUATION AND REVIEW:

What object does your sculpture represent? Show me some places where lines represent the mass of the object.

How do you like your sculpture?

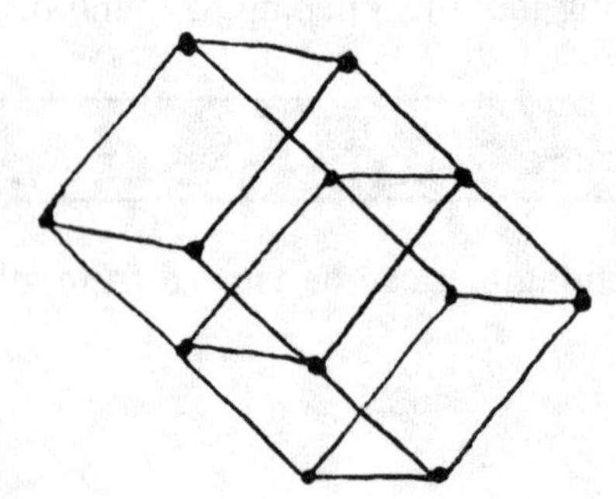

LESSON 25, YEAR C **Foil and Ink Bas Relief I** **Date** ______________

BIG IDEA: Repeated texture can create rhythm. (T2)

GOAL: The child will repeat textures to create rhythm in a foil and ink design.

MAIN ELEMENT: Texture

MATERIALS:

Sturdy piece of corrugated cardboard, approximately 12" X 15"
Pencil
Scraps of stiff material with different textures (ex., pieces of wood, emery board or nail file, lasagna noodle, screw, steel wool, etc.)
Glue
Picture of Egyptian bas relief *(from the Masterpak)* or other samples of bas relief, including coins *(optional)*

STRATEGY:

• Look at the sample(s) of bas relief. (Pronounce "bas" to rhyme with "pa". "Bas" is French for "low", and "relief" refers to being raised from a background.) Have your child look at the examples and notice how the figures "stick up" from the background.

• Explain that repeating a texture in different parts of a design can create a feeling of movement in a piece of art, which we call **rhythm.**

WORK PERIOD:

• The child chooses two or three textures that he would like to repeat to create a bas relief.

• The child then glues the textures onto the cardboard base, repeating different textures throughout the piece to create rhythm.

QUESTIONS FOR EVALUATION AND REVIEW:

Show me the different textures in your design. What does repeating textures do for your project? *(It gives the piece rhythm.)*

LESSON 26, YEAR C **Foil and Ink Bas Relief II** **Date** ____________

BIG IDEA: Repeated textures can create rhythm. (T2)

GOAL: The child will repeat textures to create rhythm in a foil and ink bas relief design.

MAIN ELEMENT: Texture

MATERIALS:

Glue
Water bowl
Brush
Aluminum foil
India ink or black tempera paint *(NOTE: A few drops of liquid dish detergent added to the paint will help it stick to the foil.)*
Paper towels
Newspaper
Smock

STRATEGY:

• Discuss the bas relief that the child made during the last session. Explain that he is going to make his bas relief more interesting.

• Demonstrate the foil and ink technique. Take your cardboard sample from last week and use a brush to cover it with glue. Place aluminum foil over the design, pressing it into the nooks and crannies of each shape. Dip a paper towel in the ink or paint and rub over the foil.

• Talk about the sample. What texture does the foil have? How does the ink change the way the foil looks? *(It emphasizes the texture, reduces shine, gives depth.)* Notice how the repeated texture all over the design gives a feeling of rhythm.

WORK PERIOD:

• The child brushes glue over his design and carefully covers it with aluminum foil. Encourage him to press the foil tightly in and around the different raised shapes.

• Next, the child rubs ink or paint into the foil, leaving more behind in the recesses and less in the raised areas. (If desired, the design can be buffed with a soft cloth to heighten the effect.)

QUESTIONS FOR EVALUATION AND REVIEW:

Explain how you created rhythm in your design. *(repeated textures)*

LESSONS 27 & 28, YEAR C **Container Sculpture** **Date** ______________

BIG IDEA: Forms occur in our environment and can be organic or man-made. (F1)

GOAL: The child will construct a non-representational form with containers.

MAIN ELEMENT: Form

MATERIALS:

Clean, empty containers of various sizes (ex., boxes, yogurt cups, juice cans, milk cartons, etc.)
Masking tape
Glue
Stapler
Tempera paints
Brushes
Water bowl
Newspaper
Smock
"Monument to the Third International" *(from the Masterpak)* or other sample of non-representational sculpture *(optional)*

STRATEGY:

- Look at the sample(s) of non-representational sculpture. (Some public buildings have pieces of modern sculpture on their lawns.)

- Talk about the similarities and differences between the modern sculpture and the paper animal sculpture your child made in Lessons 22 and 23. Both are **forms** because they can be viewed from all sides; however, the animal represents a form that occurs in nature, whereas modern sculpture is obviously man-made. This means that the animal sculpture is **representational**, while **non-representational** art does not look like anything in particular. (NOTE: Do not confuse non-representational art with abstract art. Abstract art is a separate style and is loosely representational.)

WORK PERIOD:

- Week One- The child arranges the containers into a sculpture, joining the containers with glue, tape, or staples.

- Week Two- The child paints his sculpture, using no more than three different colors.

QUESTIONS FOR EVALUATION AND REVIEW:

Tell me about your form. Is it natural or man-made? *(man-made)*

What is the difference between representational and non-representational art? *(Representational art shows real things, while non-representational art does not look like anything in particular.)*

Fabric Paint Wall Hanging

Date ____________

BIG IDEA: Repeated colors can create rhythm. (C7)

GOAL: The child will use repeating colors to create rhythm in a painted wall hanging.

MAIN ELEMENT: Color

MATERIALS:

Fabric paints (available at any craft store)
Picture frame
Piece of plain cotton fabric, about 1 inch longer and wider than the picture frame
Masking tape
Crayons
Scratch paper
Piece of cardboard the same size as the fabric

STRATEGY:

- Visit a craft store with your child and look at the fabric paints. Have your child select two or three colors that go well together. (A general rule of thumb is to keep the color families together: neons, metallics, pastels, brights, etc. Choosing colors from the same family will tend to harmonize the design.)

- At home, look at samples of patterns that have repeating colors (such as floor tiles, clothing, wallpaper, etc.). Point out how repeating colors throughout the design give a feeling of movement; this is called **rhythm** because it makes your eyes move around the work.

- Tape the cardboard to the back of the fabric to keep the fabric from shifting.

WORK PERIOD:

- The child selects crayons that match the colors of fabric paint he has chosen. He then uses these colors to experiment with different designs on scrap paper. He may want to include a small, alternating color pattern with which to "frame" the design.

- The child paints his design onto the fabric with the fabric paints.

QUESTIONS FOR EVALUATION AND REVIEW:

How do you like your shirt design?

Tell me how you chose those colors. How do they go together?

What did repeating colors do to your design? *(makes a feeling of movement; creates rhythm)*

LESSON 30, YEAR C **Diorama I** **Date** ______________

BIG IDEA: Shapes occur in our environment and can be organic or man-made. (S1)

GOAL: The child will use shapes that are natural and/or man-made in a diorama.

MAIN ELEMENT: Shape

MATERIALS:

Scissors
Construction paper
Glue
Markers
Shoe box

STRATEGY:

• Explain that a diorama is a special way to tell a story. People and "props" are cut from paper and glued into the shoe box to make the scene.

• Help your child decide on a particular scene, characters, and props. (This can be from a story he has read, from a social studies lesson, or from the Bible.) Help him determine which shapes represent natural objects and which are man-made.

• Demonstrate how to make paper tabs that can be attached to objects to make them stand up. (A simple tab to make is a small rectangle, folded in half lengthwise to make a capital "L". Glue the vertical side of the "L" to the object and the horizontal side of the "L" to the floor of the shoe box.)

WORK PERIOD:

• The child selects a scene, two or three characters, and props for his diorama. These are drawn on construction paper, colored (if desired), and cut out.

• The child lines the box with appropriate background colors. Include the sides, ceiling, and floor.

• The child cuts the various pieces and uses tabs to fasten them to the box. (NOTE: Tabs may be used to suspend props from the ceiling, such as clouds, sun or moon, balloons, birds, airplanes, kites, etc.)

Because this is a rather involved project, let your child know he has another session for adding details.

QUESTIONS FOR EVALUATION AND REVIEW:

Tell me what is happening in your diorama. Which shapes are natural (organic)? Which are man-made?

LESSON 31, YEAR C **Diorama II** **Date** ______________

BIG IDEA: Detail can emphasize main shapes. (S2)

GOAL: The child will add details to emphasize the main shapes in a diorama.

MAIN ELEMENT: Shape

MATERIALS: Same items as last session

STRATEGY:

• You may wish to review paper sculpture techniques from Lesson 25, Year B.

• Ask your child to identify the main shapes in his diorama. (These will most likely be the main characters of the story.) Point out that adding details to those shapes will make them "stand out".

• Help your child identify details that could be added to his main shapes and how it could be done. (For example, paper curls could be glued to the head of a main character to create hair.)

WORK PERIOD:

The child adds details to the main shapes in his diorama.

QUESTIONS FOR EVALUATION AND REVIEW:

How do you feel about your diorama now? Do you think it is more interesting?

When you first look at the diorama, what do you notice first? *(the main shapes)* Why do you think you notice them first? *(because they have more detail)*

LESSON 32, YEAR C — Papier Mâché Shadow Box I — Date ______________

BIG IDEA: Colors can create contrast. (C6)

GOAL: The child will use contrasting colors in a papier mâché shadow box.

MAIN ELEMENT: Color

MATERIALS:

Metylan® wallpaper paste, prepared according to package directions
Newspaper strips
Balloon
Smock
Newspaper sheets (to protect work area)
Small arrangement of plastic or dried flowers or toys

STRATEGY:

- Review with your child the concept of contrast in color (such as light and dark). Have him identify some contrasting colors around your home.

- Show the plastic or dried flowers or toys to your child. Explain that you will be using these in a shadow box that will take two sessions to complete. Ask your child to begin thinking of some colors that would contrast with the flowers or toys.

- Cover the work area with sheets of newspaper. Demonstrate the papier mâché technique.
  - Dip strips of newspaper into the paste. Draw each strip between two fingers to remove the excess.
  - Place the wet strips of newspaper over the balloon until it is covered.
  - For the succeeding layers, use a different technique. (This keeps the sculpture from getting too soggy.) Dip your fingers into the paste and tap them along a strip of newspaper. Smooth the damp strip onto the wet balloon. Continue until the second layer of newspaper strips is completed. Then rub this layer until the paste from the first layer soaks through and all lumps and air bubbles have been removed. Add paste with your fingers whenever the newspaper strips seem too dry.

WORK PERIOD:

The child uses the papier mâché process to cover the balloon with several smooth layers.

QUESTIONS FOR EVALUATION AND REVIEW:

What colors could you use to contrast with the flowers/toys?

LESSON 33, YEAR C **Papier Mâché Shadow Box II** **Date** ____________

BIG IDEA: Colors can create contrast. (C6)

GOAL: The child will use contrasting color in a papier mâché shadow box.

MAIN ELEMENT: Color

MATERIALS:

Tempera paints
Small brushes and cotton swabs
Balloon, covered with papier mâché, from last session
Smock
Newspaper sheets (to protect work area)
Water bowl
Craft gloss
Lace or other trim (in a color that contrasts with the flowers)
Glue
Sharp knife (**to be used by an adult only!**)

STRATEGY:

- Carefully cut the papier mâché balloon in half. Discard the balloon.

- Discuss possible contrasting colors that could be used on your child's papier mâché shadow box.

WORK PERIOD:

- The child paints the inside of one of the papier mâché halves with a color that will contrast with the flowers. (He may paint the outside with the same color or with a contrasting color.)

- After the paint has dried, the child seals the colors with craft gloss.

- After the craft gloss has dried, the child glues lace or other trim along the cut edge of the papier mâché. (He may also want to glue a loop of the same trim to the back of the shadow box so it can be hung.) He then glues the flowers in place inside of the shadow box.

QUESTIONS FOR EVALUATION AND REVIEW:

Why did you choose that color for your shadow box? *(It contrasted with the flowers.)*

How do you like your shadow box? Where would you like to hang it?

BIG IDEA: Lines can represent mass. (L1)

GOAL: The child will use lines to represent mass in a Paris Craft® mask.

MAIN ELEMENT: Line

MATERIALS:

Picture of West African mask *(from Masterpak)* or other masks
Paris Craft® (plaster-impregnated gauze strips used by medical personnel to make plaster casts; available at medical supply stores and some craft stores)
Aluminum foil
Newspaper
Scissors
Bowl of warm water

STRATEGY:

- Motivate your child by looking at the mask samples and discussing them. Research how masks have been used in different times and different cultures.

- Discuss with your child what kind of mask he would like to make. (It can represent a real person, or it may represent a particular character or animal.)

- Help your child make the base for his mask. Use several layers of aluminum foil to make the mask stiff. Place the foil on your child's face, quickly mold it to his features, and remove. Use scissors to carefully round off the edges of the mask.

- Demonstrate the Paris Craft® technique. Moisten strips of Paris Craft® with warm water and smooth them on top of the foil mask. Continue layering the strips until the desired thickness and size are obtained. Allow the strips to harden.

WORK PERIOD:

The child uses the Paris Craft® strips to make his mask. (Explain to your child that he will paint his mask in the next session.)

QUESTIONS FOR EVALUATION AND REVIEW:

How do you like using Paris Craft®?

What kind of mask are you going to make? What will it look like?

LESSON 35, YEAR C **Paris Craft® Mask II** **Date** ______________

BIG IDEA: Lines can represent mass. (L1)

GOAL: The child will use lines to represent mass in a Paris Craft® mask.

MAIN ELEMENT: Line

MATERIALS:

Tempera paints
Brushes of different sizes
Water bowl
Newspaper
Smock
Mask cast, from last session

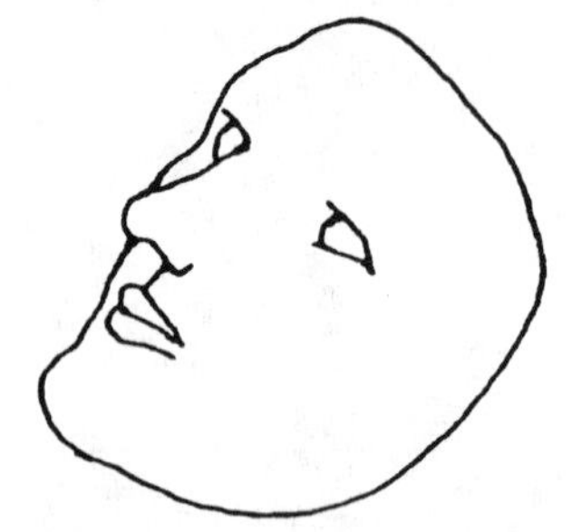

STRATEGY:

Ask your child about the kind of mask he is going to make. Discuss the different features that will be represented on the mask (such as eyebrows, lips, etc.). Help your child determine what kind of line would be appropriate for each feature.

WORK PERIOD:

- The child paints a background color on his mask and lets it dry. (Reminder: flesh tones can be made by mixing white, a little orange, and a tiny dab of blue.)

- The child uses different lines to represent different features on the mask.

QUESTIONS FOR EVALUATION AND REVIEW:

What do you think of your mask?

Show me the different lines you used. Why did you use those particular lines?

Would you make up a play to go with your mask?

LESSON _____, YEAR C   Title: ______________________________   Date ________________

OBJECTIVE:

GOAL:

MAIN ELEMENT:

MATERIALS:

STRATEGY:

WORK PERIOD:

QUESTIONS FOR EVALUATION AND REVIEW:

THE ART FIELD TRIP

When most parents think about a field trip, they think about visiting an interesting historical site, science center, aquarium, or zoo. Rarely do we link together the ideas of "art" and "field trip" in our minds. The fact remains, however, that almost any experience outside of the home school that results in learning could be classified as a "field trip". Many times great benefit can be derived from an excursion that is specifically planned in relation to art.

Why an art field trip?

Why would a parent want to plan an art field trip? If you have read through the lessons in this book, you will notice that many of them suggest visiting a particular place before beginning the actual lesson. This provides motivation for the child to continue with the art instruction. A trip to a museum or art gallery could also provide an opportunity for a parent to assess or reinforce a child's knowledge of a concept that has been taught. (For example, if you have taught the idea of contrasting colors, a visit to an exhibit of paintings could give your child an opportunity to demonstrate his understanding of the concept.) An additional benefit of a trip planned for this purpose is that children also have an opportunity to use their art vocabulary.

Another reason for an art field trip might be to find interesting subjects for drawing. Parks, zoos, city streets-- all can be exciting stimuli for a child's artistic expression. Field trips can be conducted purely for informational purposes as well. Children can learn much about career possibilities and specific techniques by observing artisans at work; also, crafts conducted in an historical setting often give fascinating glimpses into life long ago.

One of the best reasons for an art field trip, however, is to help your child develop an appreciation for art. An important first skill is to teach the child, not to glance hurriedly at a work of art and continue, but to take time to stop and **see**. Children can be taught to develop a critical eye if we as parents ask appropriate questions. For example, you may ask your child any of the following:

- Where does your eye go first in this piece? Second? Third?
- What medium was used (paint, chalk, etc.)? How would this picture be different if the artist had used a different medium?
- What technique was used? How would this picture be different if the artist had used a different technique?
- What kind of work is it (painting, print, etc.)?
- Form "picture frames" with your fingers and look at different parts of the piece. Which parts are the most interesting? Why? (Remember, with a form, you must go all the way around the piece.)
- Can you describe the piece with your eyes closed?
- What feeling does the picture give you? How would you feel if you were actually **in** the piece?
- Do you like the title of this piece? Do you think it's a good choice? Why or why not?
- What do you think the artist is trying to say?
- *(If other pieces by the same artist are being displayed)* How is this piece like the others? Different?
- How would this picture look if it were larger? Smaller? Done in a different color scheme?
- How would you change this piece, if you were the artist?

Answering questions such as these will help a child begin to think critically about art and to appreciate its unique place in the world.

<u>Places to go</u>

Many locations provide educational opportunities in the field of art. Of course, there are art museums and galleries, which may offer reduced or free admission for students. Colleges may also feature art displays, and some may allow children to observe classes.

Craft stores or fairs allow children to view pieces of useful art and sometimes provide an opportunity to see craftspeople at work. (Don't overlook historical or cultural sites, either; many have exhibits or demonstrations of crafts related to that time period or culture.) A final possibility would be private studios. All of these locations offer wonderful opportunities for art field trips, depending on your purpose.

Field trips with children

No matter how wonderful the trip you have planned, it can easily be shipwrecked by a child's inability to meet your expectations. Children have special needs that must be considered in planning a field trip of any kind.

First, children have shorter attention spans than we do. You should not plan to cover an entire museum; select just a specific display or exhibit that relates to your instructional purpose and plan to do other areas at other times. Your actual time at the field trip site should be no longer than an hour. It is also a good idea to take your child at a time of day when he is more likely to be rested and attentive (which is usually the morning hours for most children). Your child will get much more out of the trip, and, besides, it's much better for a child to leave desiring more than to leave wishing he'd never come in the first place.

Children also need structure and order; that is, they will feel more secure if they know ahead of time exactly what to expect in this new situation. It will help your child tremendously if you find out the location's rules ahead of time (such as "no touching") and explain them with any of your own before going out on your excursion. Some children (particularly those with special learning needs) also benefit if you can explain to them exactly what you will be doing. ("First we'll park in the garage, then we'll walk three blocks to the museum," etc.) Children who are given structure in this way will feel more comfortable about the field trip experience and will be more likely to concentrate on its educational aspects.

The field trip process

Never has the Boy Scout motto been truer than when planning a field trip-- "Be prepared!" You can prepare yourself for the trip by finding out as much about the location as you can beforehand. (In fact, if at all possible, visit the field trip site ahead of time to note such details as parking arrangements, cost of admission, stroller accessibility, location of rest room and/or lunch facilities, etc.) It also helps if you know exactly what you will be seeing so you can guide your child's learning more accurately. You will also want to prepare your child for the trip, as explained in the previous section.

Once you are on your way, the rule with children is "be flexible". You may want to have some games or alternate activities planned if last-minute changes should occur. Depending on the location of your field trip, a small first-aid kit and a trash bag may come in handy. While it is important to stay focused on the objective of your trip, you should feel free to follow your child's interest and attention span. (If you are visiting a craft show, for example, and you wanted your child to concentrate on the technique of weaving, do not become upset if he shows more interest in the different textiles that are being used.) If you notice that your child has become tired and has lost all interest, don't try to "stick it out" to the end. It is much better to end the field trip early than to have it be remembered as a stressful experience.

After the field trip, follow-up activities can help the child remember what was learned on the trip. Sometimes just a simple discussion (or reporting to other family members) may be all that is necessary, but you may also want to consider a follow-up project as well. For example, you may want your child to write a report about what he saw, or take a more creative tack by asking him to write a story. (Possible story topics might include "If I Were The Artist", "If I Were In This Piece of Artwork", or "What Happened in This Artwork".) He could also try to reproduce a certain artwork or technique. Following up a field trip in some form will help impress the experience into your child's mind and reinforce the learning that took place.

The world is a big place, and it contains so many interesting things to learn. Taking your child on field trips will not only reinforce what you teach in your classroom, but it will also expose your child to the many exciting experiences that lie outside your classroom door.

GLOSSARY

abstract- a shape or form taken from an actual object and altered

additive method- a method of building onto a clay sculpture by adding pieces (These pieces must be scored and moistened before attaching them to the main piece.)

bas relief- "low" sculpture, which is slightly raised from the background

base- the part of the paint that holds the pigment and binder together and makes it easy to apply

batik- a process by which a substance such as wax blocks the absorption of paint or dye into a fabric or paper

binder- the part of paint that holds the color together and "binds" it to the surface to which it is applied

blind contour drawing- a line drawing executed while looking only at the subject

collage- a collection of textures glued to a flat background

collograph- a printing plate made by gluing cardboard to a background

complementary colors- colors that are opposite on the color wheel (ex., red and green)

contour- the line around an object's edges; the thickness or width of a line

contrast- opposite in appearance, such as bright/dull, light/dark, etc.

craft- an art object created for a specific use

diorama- shapes within a box, usually depicting a scene

etching- an art form in which a design is scratched into a surface

form- a three-dimensional object, which can be viewed from all directions

landscape- a panoramic drawing or painting of the earth's natural features (excluding oceans or seas)

limited palette- a technique in which the artist limits his color choices

marbling- a technique in which color is swirled on a liquid and then applied to paper

mass- the apparent weight of an object; i.e., how heavy or light it appears to be

medium- the materials used to create an art project (such as paper, clay, etc.)

mobile- shapes or forms suspended in space

modified blind contour- a line drawing executed by looking primarily at the object

mola- a Panamanian craft in which a design is created by placing layers of fabric on top of each other and cutting the layers so that the underlying colors show through

monochromatic- artwork done in tints and shades of a single color

monoprint- a print that can be done only one time

mosaic- an art form which gets its shapes and colors from adhering many small pieces of colored stone, tile, paper, etc., to a flat base

mural- a painting or drawing which covers a wall

neutral- a color that has been "neutralized" by adding its complement

non-representational- a design not meant to suggest or represent any object; a design

organic- occurring naturally in the world around us

papier mâché- a sculpture technique in which paper strips and paste are applied to a framework

Pariscraft®- plaster-impregnated gauze used for making casts

pigment- the colored part of paint

pinch-and-pull method- a method of sculpting clay by pulling and pinching parts of a basic ball shape

Pointillism- a style of painting in which color was applied in dots

portrait- a painting or drawing of a person

representational- an art form made to look like a person or object

resist- a technique in which a substance such as oil or wax is used to prevent an area from absorbing paint

rhythm- a feeling of movement in a piece of art

sculpture- a three-dimensional piece of art

shade- created by mixing a color with black (ex., hunter green, maroon)

shape- a flat object; that is, it has only two dimensions (ex., circle, square)

space- the feeling of depth in a piece of art

squeegee- a flat object whose side is scraped across a wet surface

stencil- a shape cut from cardboard, used to repeat that shape in an art piece

still life- a drawing or painting of arranged objects

texture- the degree of roughness or smoothness that an object has

tint- created by mixing a color with white (ex., pink, lavender)

tool- an object used by the hand to create an art project (ex., pencil, brush)

warp- the threads that make up the framework of a weaving

weft- in weaving, the threads which are woven over and under the warp

BIBLIOGRAPHY

Arnold, Arnold. The Crowell Book of Arts and Crafts for Children. New York: Thomas Y. Crowell Co., 1975.

Brookes, Mona. Drawing With Children. Los Angeles: Jeremy P. Tucker, 1986.

Edwards, Betty. Drawing on the Right Side of the Brain. Los Angeles: J. P. Tucker, 1979.

Gaitskell, Charles D; Al Hurwitz, and Michael Day. Children and Their Art. New York: Harcourt, Brace, and Javonovich, 1982.

Jenkins, Peggy D. Art for the Fun of It. Englewood Cliffs, NJ: Prentice-Hall, Inc., 1980.

Linderman, Earl W., and Marlene M. Arts and Crafts for the Classroom. New York: MacMillan, 1977.

Linderman, Marlene M. Art in the Elementary School. Dubuque, IA: William C. Brown Publishers, 1984.

Solga, Kim. Build Art! Cincinnati: North Light Books, 1992.

Solga, Kim. Draw! Cincinnati: North Light Books, 1991.

Solga, Kim. Make Gifts! Cincinnati: North Light Books, 1991.

Solga, Kim. Make Prints! Cincinnati: North Light Books, 1991.

Solga, Kim. Make Sculptures! Cincinnati: North Light Books, 1992.

Solga, Kim. Paint! Cincinnati: North Light Books, 1991.

Wachowiak, Frank, and Theodore Ramsey. Emphasis: Art. New York: Intext Educational Publishers, 1971.

INDEX

The following index will help you select lessons that can be incorporated into a unit-study curriculum. A topic is given, followed by the lesson number which relates to the topic.

Aluminum 12A, 25C, 26C

Animals 23A, 24A, 34A, 25B, 22C, 23C

Arp, Hans (Jean) 17C

Attitudes 6A, 13A, 14A, 2B, 3B, 25B

Bas relief 27A, 28A, 25C, 26C

Batik 19A

Bayeux Tapestry 18A

Bubbles 12C

Cartoons (comics) 2B, 3B, 8C

Chalk 18A

Cities 3C

Clay 22A, 23A, 24A, 10B, 27B, 28B

Clothing 11A, 34A, 33B

Collage 12B, 17C

Collograph 13A, 14A

Complementary colors 17A, 29A, 23B, 34B, 35B, 12C

de la Tour, Georges 16B

Diorama 30C, 31C

Dove, Arthur 16C

Dürer, Albrecht 12A

Dyeing 33B

Emotions 6A, 13A, 14A, 2B, 3B, 25B

England (history) 18A

Feelings 6A, 13A, 14A, 2B, 3B, 25B

Food 22B, 24C

Fruit 22B

Gadgets 11A

Imagination 4A

Indians (Native Americans) 31A, 27B, 28B

Insects 4B

Kandinsky, Wassily 13A

Klee, Paul 13A

Masks 34C, 35C

Mobiles 26B

Mola (Panama) 29B, 30B

Mondrian (artist) 13A

Mosaic 15C, 15B, 31B, 32B

Mural 17B, 18B

Nature study 8A, 8B, 7C

Neutral colors 24A, 16B, 9C

Non-representational art 13A, 17A, 17C, 27C, 28C

Oil 16A, 9B

O'Keefe, Georgia 16C

Panama 29B, 30B

Papier mâché 32C, 33C

Peas 24C

Picasso, Pablo 16C

Placemat 29A

Plaster 27A, 28A

Pointillism 8C

Pollock 13A, 20A

Popcorn 22B

Portraits 6B, 6C, 20C, 21C

Pottery 32A, 33A, 27B, 28B

Puppets 34A

Rembrandt 16B

Rocks 23B

Rome (ancient) 15C

Sand 27A, 28A, 31A

Sandpaper 3A, 20B, 8C

Seurat, Georges 8C

Sewing 22B

Shades 15A, 15B, 16C

Shadows 32C, 33C

Shoe box 30C, 31C

Socks 34A

South America 29B, 30B

Stained glass 9A

Stationery 9B

Still life 2A, 1B, 4C, 5C, 18C, 19C

Textiles 11A, 34A, 22B, 34B, 35B, 29C

Textures 3A, 11A, 20A, 21A, 23A, 12B, 20B, 31B, 32B, 8C, 25C, 26C

Tints 15A, 15B, 16C

Tissue paper 15C

Toothpicks 24C

Van Gogh, Vincent 16A, 20A

Vermeer, Jan 16B

Weaving 29A, 30A, 34B, 35B

Woodcuts 12A

Wrapping paper 35A, 9B

AT HOME PUBLICATIONS

This book is published by At Home Publications, a family business dedicated to meeting curriculum needs. We also publish Early Education at Home, a curriculum guide for preschool and kindergarten, and the Masterpak, a set of 40 art reproductions to supplement the Art Adventures at Home series.

To order additional materials, please complete the information below.

Name ____

Address ____

____

Age(s) of children ____________________ Phone ____________________

Item(s) ordered:

____ Early Education at Home @ $24.95 each ________

____ Art Adventures at Home, Level 1 *(gr. K-2)* @ $24.95 each ________

____ Art Adventures at Home, Level 2 *(gr.* 3-5) @ $24.95 each ________

____ Art Adventures at Home, Level 3 *(gr.* 6-8) @ $24.95 each ________

____ Masterpak @ $15.00 each ________

SUBTOTAL ________

Add shipping and handling +$5.00

TOTAL ________

Send with check or money order made payable to At Home Publications, 2834 Grier Nursery Road, Forest Hill, MD 21050. Questions? Call or fax (410) 420-2230 or email athomepubs@juno.com.